Better Homes and Gardens®
DESIGNERS & Their
QUILTS

39

80

101

51

45

67

Contents

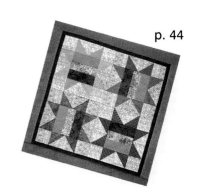

p. 44

The Quilts of Our Times.

The 16 designers featured in this book have defined some of this era's most memorable quilt styles. From the precision of Tess Herlan's English paper piecing to the gentle lines of Joined at the Hip folk art, each designer explores a different facet of this heirloom art.

There are projects to delight virtually every taste in this compilation of their work. Specific materials lists, step-by-step instructions, and understandable placement diagrams and illustrations will help you complete each project as quickly and as easily as possible. From fabric selection to finishing, this is the information you need to succeed.

So go ahead. Pick up a few pieces and do a little patchwork.

Happy Quilting!

p. 30

Cindy BLACKBERG

Artist Cindy Blackberg enriches patchwork with her signature small-stitch quilting. In "Trafalgar Charm," *opposite*, she explores Nelson's Victory, a traditional block that echoes a battleship formation used in the 1805 Battle of Trafalgar. Hundreds of scraps honor the late-1800s charm quilt tradition of using a fabric only once. Her plaid Sawtooth block, *left*, illustrates another tradition of that time.

"When you can do something that you really love, a hobby turned into a job, it's wonderful."

—Cindy Blackberg

She started with Sunbonnet Sue and Overall Sam appliqué patterns, making a small quilt of four huge blocks.

"It still has charm for me," Cindy Blackberg says of her 1974 effort. "Big blocks are very encouraging to beginners. Since then I've learned that I love pieced quilts more."

"My work is tradition based; sometimes I put my own spin on it."

—Cindy Blackberg

She's developed her own design style in the process. The elongation of a favorite block, the Sawtooth Star, resulted in Yankee Doodle, her first published pattern.

"I enjoy the teaching part almost as much as I enjoy the quilting," says Cindy, who began teaching when she moved with her family to Florida. She couldn't find a quilting class to take, so this self-taught quilter began teaching others to quilt.

In 1993, just 15 years after teaching that first class, Cindy earned the Jewel Pearce Patterson award, an honor given in recognition of the fourth-generation Texas quilter and quilt teacher.

"That opened a large opportunity for me," Cindy says. "Now I teach hand piecing and hand quilting nationally and internationally."

These days, when she isn't teaching, "I'm sitting here working," she says. One facet of her work is accommodating quilters' need to make hand piecing easier and more accurate. In that vein, she manufactures template stamps with lines for both cutting and piecing. With this tool, quilters can stamp the template on the wrong side of the fabric, then use the outside line for cutting and the inside line for piecing.

TRAFALGAR CHARM

Materials

6 yards total of assorted light, medium, and dark prints
3 yards of blue print for inner and outer borders
3 yards of solid blue for middle border
1 yard of solid black for binding
6 yards of backing fabric
74×98" of quilt batting

Finished quilt top: 71×95"
Finished block: 4×6"

Quantities specified for 44/45"-wide, 100% cotton fabrics. All measurements include a ¼" seam allowance. Sew with right sides together unless otherwise stated.

Select the Fabrics

Trafalgar Charm resembles quilts made during the late 1800s. The "charm" was not to repeat any of the fabrics.

When selecting fabrics for your charm quilt, choose an assortment of light, medium, and dark prints for contrast. Avoid busy prints because they distract from the pattern forming in the quilt.

To create more interest in the quilt top, substitute the medium-color fabric for both the dark and light fabrics. For example, use the medium-color fabric instead of a dark fabric when placed near light fabric, and use the medium-color fabric instead of a light fabric when placed near a dark fabric.

Cut the Fabrics

To make the best use of your fabrics, cut the pieces in the order that follows.

The pattern is on *page 129*. To make a template of the pattern, follow the instructions in Quilting Basics, which begins on *page 113*. Be sure to transfer the dots marked on the patterns to the templates, then to the fabric pieces. The dots are the matching points and are needed to set in seams.

Helpful Hint: Place light fabrics for one unit with right sides together. Cut both a Charm Pattern and Charm reversed pattern at one time. Repeat with dark fabrics for one unit.

The border strips are cut lengthwise (parallel to the selvage). Extra length has been added to the strips to allow for mitering the borders.

From assorted light prints, cut:
- 144 *each* of Charm Pattern and Charm Pattern reversed

From assorted dark prints, cut:
- 144 *each* of Charm Pattern and Charm Pattern reversed

From blue print, cut:
- 2—4×100″ strips for outer border
- 2—4×77″ strips for outer border
- 2—2¾×78″ strips for inner border
- 2—2¾×54″ strips for inner border

From solid blue, cut:
- 2—6½×92″ strips for middle border
- 2—6½×68″ strips for middle border

From solid black, cut:
- 9—2½×42″ binding strips

Assemble the Blocks

When assembling this block, you'll need to set in seams. The key to setting angled pieces together is aligning marked matching points carefully. Whether you're stitching by machine or hand, start and stop sewing precisely at the matching points. This is an instance where it's necessary to backstitch to secure the ends of the seams. It prepares the angle for the next piece to be set in.

1. Pin together a dark print piece and a dark print piece reversed. Carefully align the matching points (see Diagram 1). Sew together, being sure not to sew into the ¼″ seam allowances, to make a dark unit. Pin together a light print piece and a light print piece reversed. Sew together the pieces to make a light unit.

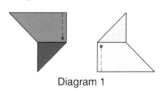

Diagram 1

2. Referring to Diagram 2 for placement, align the matching points along seam No. 1. Sew together, being sure not to sew into the ¼″ seam allowance. Then join the remaining seams, sewing from the inside toward the outside to make a block A (see Diagram 3). Press the seam allowances open. Pieced block A should measure 4½×6½″, including the seam allowances.

Diagram 2 Diagram 3

3. Repeat steps 1 and 2 to make a total of 72 of block A.

4. In the same manner as for making block A, make block B by rotating the position of the Charm Pattern pieces (see diagrams 4 and 5). Repeat to make a total of 72 of block B.

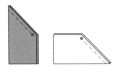

Diagram 4 Diagram 5

Assemble the Quilt Top

1. Referring to the Quilt Assembly Diagram for placement, lay out the blocks in 18 horizontal rows.

2. Sew together the blocks in each row. Press the seam allowances in one direction, alternating the direction with each row. Then join the rows to make the quilt center. Press the seam allowances in one direction. The pieced quilt center should measure 48½×72½", including the seam allowances.

Add the Borders

1. Aligning long edges and centering the strips, sew together one blue print 2³⁄₄×54" strip, one solid blue 6½×68" strip, and one blue print 4×77" strip to make a top border strip unit. Press the seam allowances toward the solid blue strip. Repeat to make a bottom border strip unit.

2. Aligning long edges and centering the strips, sew together one blue print 2³⁄₄×78" strip, one solid blue 6½×92" strip, and one

Quilt Assembly Diagram

blue print 4×100" strip to make a side border strip unit. Press the seam allowances toward the solid blue strip. Repeat to make a second side border strip unit.

3. Add the border strip units to the pieced quilt center using mitered corners to complete the quilt top. For assistance in mitering corners, refer to Quilting Basics, which begins on *page 113*.

Complete the Quilt

1. Layer the quilt top, batting, and backing according to the instructions in Quilting Basics, which begin on *page 113*. Quilt as desired.

2. Use the solid black 1½×42" strips to bind the quilt according to instructions in Quilting Basics. ■

Joined
AT THE HIP

Joined at the Hip designers

Avis Shirer, *far left*, and Tammy

Johnson celebrate nature with

gentle humor. "Pumpkin

Stars," *opposite*, is a prime

example of their distinctive

look, a combination of

friendly folk art appliqué with

geometric patchwork.

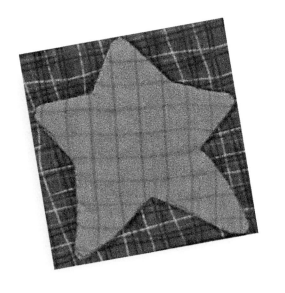

"We gravitate toward simple shapes that the needle seems to just naturally follow."

—Avis Shirer

Folk art created with an abundance of fabrics is their hallmark. Tammy Johnson and Avis Shirer, the creative team known as Joined at the Hip, have an open mind when it comes to combining prints with plaids, even in a controlled color scheme.

"We'll start with two or three fabrics, and just keep adding," Avis says. "It's a more forgiving quilt when you have a huge variety of fabrics, because you can use so many different shades of the same color."

They often slip in a fabric "that was so ugly, we had to buy it," Tammy says.

"Often times, that's the one piece that everybody will comment about."

—Avis Shirer

When quilt lovers look at a finished Joined at the Hip piece, the odd-ball textile is often the one they notice and compliment.

"On the bolt, that's the fabric that wouldn't get a second glance from most quilters," Avis says.

The duo met when they both worked at the Farmer's Co-op in the hamlet of Britt, Iowa. Now this prolific pair has been designing primitive folk art for quilters for two decades.

"Life is short. Enjoy it."

—Tammy Johnson

They continue to take delight in creating projects that reflect their life in the heartland; quilt projects that combine patchwork with appliqué for flavorful folk art results.

PUMPKIN STARS

Materials
⅓ yard of light tan print for pumpkin
    appliqué foundation
¼ yard of light olive green print for
    inner border
Scraps of assorted purple, green,
    brown, and rust prints for triangle-
    squares, star appliqué foundations,
    and pumpkin appliqués
3—9×10" rectangles of assorted
    orange prints for pumpkin appliqués
Scraps of two dark orange prints for
    pumpkin appliqués
Scraps of light orange print for
    pumpkin appliqués
13" square of dark green print for
    vine appliqué
6—4½" squares of gold prints for
    star appliqués
¼ yard of olive green print for binding
30×28" of quilt batting
30×28" of backing fabric

Finished quilt top: 24×22"

Quantities specified for 44/45"-wide,
100% cotton fabrics. All measurements
include a ¼" seam allowance. Sew
with right sides together unless
otherwise stated.

Cut the Fabrics
To make the best use of your fabrics, cut
the pieces in the order that follows.

From light tan print, cut:
■ 1—10½×20½″ rectangle for appliqué
    foundation
From light olive green print, cut:
■ 2—2½×20½″ inner border strips
■ 2—2½×14½″ inner border strips
*From assorted purple, green, brown, and rust prints,
cut:*
■ 6—4⅞″ squares, cutting each in half
    diagonally for a total of 12 triangles
■ 6—4½″ squares for appliqué foundations
From olive green print, cut:
■ 3—2½×42″ binding strips

Assemble the Quilt
1. Aligning raw edges, sew the light olive
green print 2½×20½″ inner border strips
to the side edges of the light tan print
10½×20½″ rectangle. Then add the light
olive green print 2½×14½″ inner border
strips to the top and bottom edges of the
light tan print rectangle to make the quilt
center. Press all seam allowances toward
the light olive green print inner border.

2. Join two assorted print triangles to make
a triangle-square (see Triangle-Square
Diagram). Press the seam allowance in one
direction. The pieced triangle-square
should measure 4½″ square, including the
seam allowances. Repeat to make a total of
six triangle-squares.

Triangle-Square Diagram

3. Referring to the photograph *opposite* for
placement, lay out the six assorted purple,
green, brown, and rust print 4½″ squares
and the six triangle-squares in two rows.

4. Sew together the squares in each row to
make two outer border strips. Press the
seam allowances in one direction. Each
pieced outer border strip should measure
4½×24½″, including the seam allowances.
Join the outer border strips to the top and
bottom edges of the quilt center to
complete the quilt top. Press the seam
allowances toward the light olive green
inner border.

Appliqué the Quilt Center
The patterns are on *page 128*. To make
templates of the patterns, follow the
instructions in Quilting Basics, which
begins on *page 113*.

From brown print scraps, cut:
■ 1 *each* of patterns A, F, and K
From orange print rectangles, cut:
■ 1 *each* of patterns B, G, and L
From dark orange print scraps, cut:
■ 1 *each* of patterns C, D, E, M, N, and O
From light orange print scraps, cut:
■ 1 *each* of patterns H, I, and J
From dark green print, cut:
■ 1—12″ square, cutting it into enough
    2″-wide bias strips to total 72″ in length
    (For specific instructions on cutting
    bias strips, see Quilting Basics.)
From gold print squares, cut:
■ 6 of Pattern P

1. Referring to the photograph *opposite* for
placement, position the pumpkin appliqué
pieces on the light tan print rectangle.
Position the gold print P stars
on the outer border squares. Baste all
pieces in place.

2. Using threads in colors that match the
fabrics, appliqué the pieces to the
foundations. Always work from the bottom
layer to the top.

3. Finger-press under ³/₁₆″ along the long edges of the dark green print 72″-long bias strip to make the vine.

4. Position the prepared vine on the inner border. Using thread in a color that matches the fabric, appliqué the vine in place.

Complete the Quilt

1. Layer the quilt top, batting, and backing according to the instructions in Quilting Basics, which begins on *page 113*. Quilt as desired.

2. Use the olive green print 2¹/₂×42″ strips to bind the quilt according to the instructions in Quilting Basics. ■

Shar JORGENSON

For many quilters, a perfect Mariner's Compass is a lifetime achievement because of the challenges of cutting accurate pieces and piecing sharp points. Shar Jorgenson's suggestions help simplify this seafaring project, *opposite*. Try it and see for yourself; use the color palette Shar used, the sample color scheme, *left*, or your favorite hues.

"If I'm going to do it, I'm going to do it right."

—Shar Jorgenson

Quilting is a family affair for Sharlene Jorgenson. Like her mother, grandmother, and great-grandmother before her, Shar hosted quilting bees when her children were growing up and pieced with friends to pass the time.

In fact, it was while she was piecing around a picnic table with friends that Shar decided to begin producing and selling her own quilt products and patterns. She was working on a Double Wedding Ring project at the time and was frustrated because she couldn't find a suitable template. She had one made and liked it so much, a business was launched.

Now Shar's trademark rose-color templates, laser-cut of sturdy plexiglass, assure .0001" accuracy on the most intricate of patterns.

"I only wanted to have fun making quilts."

—Shar Jorgenson

Shar is still hosting quilting bees, but on television. Instead of chatting with friends around a quilting frame, she is a living-room guest in homes across the nation. Her public television program introduces the joy of quilting one step at a time.

She inspires experienced quilters with innovative, timesaving ideas, and coaxes beginners with friendly advice. And she embraces the appeal of every color option.

"Mom has that traditional designing that people just love," says daughter Angela Jorgenson, her co-host. "I tend to go a little more toward the funky. We give them two very different options, Mom's and mine."

"She has a thorough way of explaining things. And her templates make it so anybody can quilt quickly and perfectly."

MARINER'S COMPASS

Materials

1½ yards of red-and-green leaf print for blocks, border, and binding

1¼ yards of tan print with gold for blocks and setting squares

⅛ yard of gold print for blocks

⅝ yard of dark green print for blocks and border

½ yard of green print for blocks

½ yard of dark red print for blocks

⅜ yard of red-and-gold print for blocks

2⅜ yards of backing fabric

56" square of quilt batting

Finished quilt top: 50" square
Finished block: 12" square

Quantities specified for 44/45"-wide, 100% cotton fabrics. All measurements include a ¼" seam allowance. Sew with right sides together unless otherwise stated.

Cut the Fabrics

To make the best use of your fabrics, cut the pieces in the order that follows.

The pattern pieces are on *page 123*. To make templates from the patterns, follow the instructions in Quilting Basics, which begins on *page 113*.

From red-and-green leaf print, cut:
- 6—2½×42" binding strips
- 4—6½×38½" border strips
- 1—1⅜×20" strip for Block 1
- 8 of Pattern C for blocks 3 and 5
- 4 of Pattern D for Block 2
- 1 of Pattern E for Block 4
- 4 of Pattern I for Block 6
- 4 of Pattern I reversed for Block 6

From tan print with gold, cut:
- 4—12½" setting squares
- 20 of Pattern I for blocks 1 through 6
- 20 of Pattern I reversed for blocks 1 through 6
- 32 of Pattern A for blocks 1 and 5
- 128 of Pattern F for blocks 2, 3, 4, and 6

From gold print, cut:
- 1—1½×26" strip for Block 1
- 1—1½×14" strip for Block 3
- 8 of Pattern H for Block 5

From dark green print, cut:
- 2—1½×38½" border strips
- 2—1½×36½" border strips
- 1—2⅜×22" strip for Block 3
- 1—1⅛×38" strip for Block 1
- 32 of Pattern G for blocks 2 and 6
- 8 of Pattern C for blocks 3 and 4
- 1 of Pattern E for Block 5

From green print, cut:
- 1—1⅛×38" strip for Block 1
- 1—1¾×22" strip for Block 3
- 24 of Pattern B for blocks 2, 5, and 6
- 16 of Pattern G for Block 4

From dark red print, cut:
- 1—1⅜×20" strip for Block 1
- 8 of Pattern H for Block 3
- 12 of Pattern D for blocks 4 and 6

From red-and-gold print, cut:
- 1—1½×26" strip for Block 1
- 1—3⅜×14" strip for Block 3
- 12 of Pattern C for blocks 2, 5, and 6
- 8 of Pattern B for Block 4
- 1 of Pattern E for Block 3

Assemble Block 1

1. With long raw edges aligned, sew together the gold print 1½×26" strip and the red-and-gold print 1½×26" strip. Press the seam allowances open. Align the pattern piece with the seam line of the strip set to create a shadow (see Photo 1). Cutting half of the points facing in opposite directions can create even more shadow variations (see Photo 2).

Photo 1

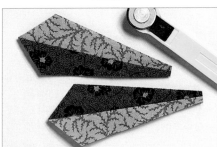

Photo 2

2. Cut four of Pattern D from the strip set.

3. Repeat steps 1 and 2 with the red-and-green leaf print 1⅜×20" strip and the dark red print 1⅜×20" strip; cut four of Pattern

C from the strip set. Then cut eight of Pattern B from a strip set composed of the dark green print 1¹/₈×38″ strip and the green print 1¹/₈×38″ strip.

4. Arrange the B, C, and D pieces from the previous steps, 16 tan print with gold A pieces, four tan print with gold I pieces, and four tan print with gold I reversed pieces on a flannel board for Block 1 (see Diagram 1).

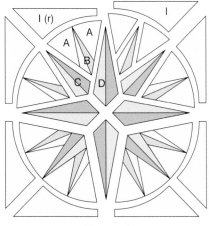

Diagram 1
Block 1

As you prepare to sew, start from the outside edge of the circle with the smallest pieces and working toward the center, graduating to a larger point each time.

5. Join an A piece and B piece with the B piece on top (see Diagram 2). The pieces should meet ¹/₄″ from the edge. The ears are not equal in size. The sides of the points are on the bias, so handle them as little as possible. Do not backstitch on either end.

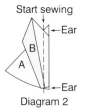

Diagram 2

Turn the unit to the right side. Finger-press the seam allowance to one side before you press with an iron. Scratch the fabric as you run your index finger along the seam, moving the seam allowance away from the B piece. This makes it easier to maintain a sharp point. Then press the seam allowance with an iron; cut off the ears. Using the same technique, add the second A piece to complete this unit. Repeat to make a total of 8 A/B/A units (see Diagram 3).

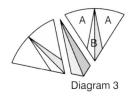

Diagram 3

6. Add a C piece to one side of an A/B/A unit (see Diagram 3). It's easier to control the bias edges if you start sewing at the wide end. Press the seam allowance away from the C piece as previously directed. Then add a second A/B/A unit to the other side of the C piece in the same manner. Repeat to make a total of four units.

7. Add a D piece to a unit from Step 6 (see Diagram 4), beginning ¹/₄″ from the center and sewing toward the narrow end. Add a second unit to the other side of the D piece. Make a total of two units.

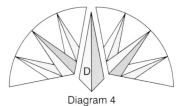

Diagram 4

8. Set in a D piece in each unit from Step 7 (see Diagram 5). Stitch from the center toward the narrow end. To finish the center of the compass, start sewing at one dot (see Diagram 5) and sew toward the

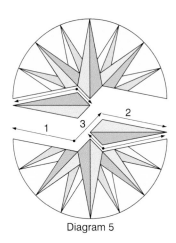

Diagram 5

outside of the block. Repeat on the other side of the block. Then sew between the dots. To help reduce bulk, press half of the seams in one direction and half in the other direction.

9. Join one I piece and one I reversed piece. Repeat for a total of four pairs.

10. Connect the four pairs to form a frame (see Diagram 6). Press the seam allowances open.

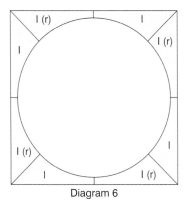

Diagram 6

11. Match the points of the compass to the seams of the frame. Note the direction of the compass arrows before stitching.

Join the two pieces with the I pieces on the bottom so the intersections of the compass are visible. Sew directly over the

MARINER'S COMPASS

intersections for perfect points on the right side. Press the seam allowances toward the outside of the block. Pieced Block 1 should measure 12½″ square, including the seam allowances.

Assemble Block 2

1. Arrange four red-and-green leaf print D pieces, four red-and-gold print C pieces, eight green print B pieces, 16 dark green print G pieces, 32 tan print with gold F pieces, four tan print with gold I pieces, and four tan print with gold I reversed pieces on a flannel board for Block 2 (see Diagram 7).

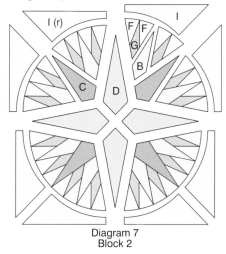

Diagram 7
Block 2

2. Following the sewing instructions as previously given for Block 1, start sewing together the smallest pieces on the outside and work toward the center and larger pieces. Pieced Block 2 should measure 12½″ square, including the seam allowances.

Assemble Block 3

1. With long raw edges aligned, join the red-and-gold print 3⅜×14″ strip and the gold print 1½×14″ strip. To create concentric circles in a block, align the outside points of the pattern piece with the seam line of the strip set (see Photo 3). Cut eight of Pattern B from the strip set.

Photo 3

With long raw edges aligned, join the dark green print 2⅜×22″ strip and the green print 1¾×22″ strip. Align the outside tips of Pattern G with the seam line of the strip set; cut 16 of Pattern G.

2. Arrange the B and G pieces from the previous step, four dark green print C pieces, four red-and-green leaf print C pieces, one red-and-gold print E circle, eight dark red print H pieces, 32 tan print with gold F pieces, four tan print with gold I pieces, and four tan print with gold I reversed pieces on a flannel board for Block 3 (see Diagram 8).

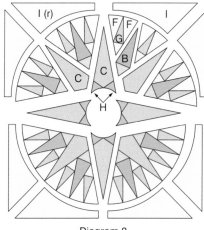

Diagram 8
Block 3

3. Match the edges of a dark red print H piece and a dark green print C piece (see Diagram 9). Do not backstitch at either end of this seam. Finger-press first, then

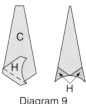

Diagram 9

press with an iron. Repeat this step when adding a second H to the other side of the C piece. Repeat in this manner with the remaining three dark green print C pieces and the remaining six dark red print H pieces.

4. Following the sewing instructions as previously given for Block 1, start sewing the smallest pieces on the outside and work toward the center and larger pieces. Pieced Block 3 should measure 12½″ square, including the seam allowances.

5. To prepare the red-and-gold print center E circle for appliqué, turn under a ¼″ seam allowance around the edge of the circle and baste. Pin the circle in place on the block, making sure the edge of the circle touches the points of the compass. With a matching thread, blindstitch the circle in place.

Assemble Block 4

1. Arrange one red-and-green leaf print E circle, four dark red print D pieces, four dark green print C pieces, eight red-and-gold print B pieces, 16 green print G pieces, 32 tan print with gold F pieces, four tan print with gold I pieces, and four tan print with gold I reversed pieces on a flannel board for Block 4 (see Diagram 10).

2. Following the sewing instructions as previously given for Block 1, start joining the smallest pieces on the outside and work toward the center and larger pieces. Finally, appliqué the center E circle over the D pieces. Pieced Block 4 should measure 12½″ square, including the seam allowances.

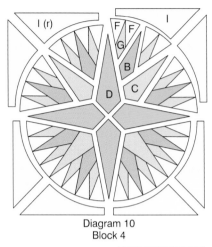

Diagram 10
Block 4

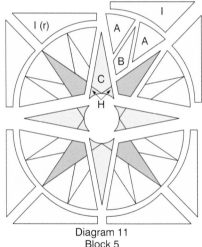

Diagram 11
Block 5

Assemble Block 5

1. Arrange one dark green print E circle, four red-and-green leaf print C pieces, eight gold print H pieces, four red-and-gold print C pieces, eight green print B pieces, 16 tan print with gold A pieces, four tan print with gold I pieces, and four tan print with gold I reversed pieces on a flannel board for Block 5 (see Diagram 11).

2. Following the sewing instructions as previously given for Block 1, start sewing the smallest pieces on the outside and work toward the center and larger pieces. Then appliqué the center E circle over the

center of the block. Pieced Block 5 should measure 12½" square, including the seam allowances.

Assemble Block 6

1. Arrange two dark red print D pieces, one red-and-gold print C piece, two green print B pieces, four dark green print G pieces, eight tan print with gold F pieces, one red-and-green leaf print I piece, and one red-and-green leaf print I reversed piece on a flannel board for Block 6 (see Diagram 12).

2. Following the sewing instructions as previously given for Block 1, join the smallest pieces on the outside and work toward the center and larger pieces. Trim the block to 6½" square, including the seam allowances (see Diagram 13).

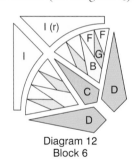

Diagram 12
Block 6

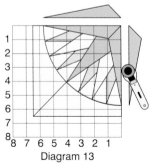

Diagram 13

3. Repeat steps 1 and 2 to make a total of four blocks.

Assemble the Quilt Center

1. Referring to the photograph on *page 17* for placement, lay out the five Mariner's

Compass blocks and four 12½" setting squares. Sew together the blocks in each row. Press the seam allowances in each row in the same direction, alternating with each row.

2. Join the rows to complete the quilt center. The pieced quilt center should measure 36½" square, including the seam allowances.

Add the Borders

1. Sew the dark green print 1½×36½" border strips to opposite edges of the quilt center. Then add the dark green print 1 ½×38 ½" border strips to the remaining edges of the quilt center. Press the seam allowances toward the border strips.

2. Join the red-and-green leaf print 6½×38½" border strips to opposite edges of the quilt top. Then add one Block 6 to each end of the remaining border strips. Sew the strips to the remaining edges of the quilt top. Press the seam allowances toward the border strips.

Complete the Quilt

1. Layer the quilt top, batting, and backing according to the instructions in Quilting Basics, which begins on *page 113*. Quilt as desired.

2. Use the red-and-green leaf print 2 ½×42" strips to bind the quilt according to the instructions in Quilting Basics. ■

Little
QUILTS

This trio of talented designers —Sylvia Johnson, Alice Berg, and Mary Ellen Von Holt, *left to right*, collectively known as Little Quilts— pursue patterns for small scrap quilts that look old. They prefer appliqué that is more folk art than fine and have a healthy respect for traditional patterns. Their "Birthday Baskets" quilt, *opposite*, celebrates spring in vintage reproduction prints.

"We add a surprise of color, just as we'd add a little spice to a recipe."

—Alice Berg

At Little Quilts, success is measured by the inch, as snippets of fabric become small works of old-fashioned art. The cheerful "Little Quilts look," as some quilters call it, is a combination of light, medium, and dark shades of each color in the palette stitched together in a small, though not miniature, quilt.

It all began in the early 1980s, when friends Mary Ellen Von Holt and Alice Berg spent hours ogling photos of antique furnishings. Captivated by the tiny quilts they saw in the magazines, they were determined to re-create them.

"We were obsessed with finding the best way to create these small quilts."

—Mary Ellen Von Holt

"We tried stencils, coffee stains—even a secret recipe for dyeing with tobacco juice and ammonia [to get an aged appearance]," Mary Ellen says. After weeks of testing, they succeeded. It was then that another friend, Sylvia Johnson, joined them to help create and market the small, antique-looking quilts.

Their quilts were an immediate hit. They set off a wave of interest in small-size projects, and assigned to quilts a new level of importance in home decor.

When the designers glimpsed a woman secretly tracing one of their designs during a local show, they realized a new dream. "It came to us," Alice says, "that with a kit, customers could reproduce our quilts with our approval."

With that, Little Quilts grew from creating custom quilts to designing them. Today the trio also designs fabrics, authors books, and owns a successful quilt shop.

Still, as Sylvia points out, one thing remains the same: "We like to make new quilts that look old."

"The Little Heart Quilt" launched Little Quilts' kit business.

BIRTHDAY BASKETS

Materials for Quilt

9—5½" squares of assorted light
 prints for appliqué foundations
9—5" squares of assorted pink, yellow,
 blue, and purple prints for basket
 appliqués
4—⅛-yard pieces of assorted pink
 prints for border
¼ yard of off-white print for border
¼ yard of pink print for binding
22" square of backing fabric
22" square of thin quilt batting
Embroidery floss: black

Finished quilt top: 18" square
Finished block: 5" square

Quantities specified for 44/45"-wide,
100% cotton fabrics. All measurements
include a ¼" seam allowance. Sew
with right sides together unless
otherwise stated.

Cut the Fabrics

To make the best use of your fabrics, cut
the pieces in the order that follows. The
patterns are on *page 129*. To make a template
of the basket pattern, follow the
instructions in Quilting Basics, which
begins on *page 113*.

*From each assorted pink, yellow, blue, or purple
print, cut:*
■ 1 of Pattern A
From assorted pink prints, cut:
■ 22—2⅜" squares, cutting each in half
 diagonally for a total of 44 triangles
From off-white print, cut:
■ 22—2⅜" squares, cutting each in half
 diagonally for a total of 44 triangles
From pink print, cut:
■ 2—2½×42" binding strips

Appliqué the Blocks

Using the black embroidery floss and a
blanket stitch, appliqué an assorted pink,
yellow, blue, or purple basket shape to each
assorted light print 5½" square.

 To blanket stitch, pull your needle up at
A (see diagram *below*), form a reverse L
shape with the floss, and hold the angle of
the L shape in place with your thumb. Push
the needle down at B and come up at C to
secure the stitch. Continue in the same
manner.

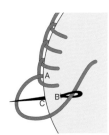

Blanket Stitch

Assemble the Quilt Center

1. Referring to the photograph on *page 25*
for placement, lay out the appliquéd blocks
in three horizontal rows.

2. Sew together the squares in each row.
Press the seam allowances in one direction,
alternating the direction with each row.
Then join the rows to make the quilt
center. Press the seam allowances in one
direction. The quilt center should measure
15½" square, including seam allowances.

Assemble and Add the Border

1. Sew together one pink print triangle
and one off-white print triangle to make
a triangle-square (see Triangle-Square
Diagram). Press the seam allowance
toward the pink triangle. The pieced
triangle-square should measure 2" square,
including the seam allowances. Repeat to
make a total of 44 triangle-squares.

Triangle-Square Diagram

2. Sew together 10 triangle-squares in a
row to make a border strip. Repeat to
make a second border strip. Sew the border
strips to opposite edges of the quilt center.
Press the seam allowances toward the
quilt center.

3. Sew together 12 triangle-squares in a
row to make a border strip. Repeat to
make a second border strip. Sew the border
strips to the remaining edges of the quilt
center to complete the quilt top. Press the
seam allowances toward the quilt center.

Complete the Quilt

1. Layer the quilt top, batting, and
backing according to the instructions in
Quilting Basics, which begins on *page 113*.
Quilt as desired.

2. Use the pink print 2½×42" strips to
bind the quilt according to the instructions
in Quilting Basics.

Materials for Pillow

5½" square of light pink print for appliqué foundation
5" square of pink print No. 1 for basket appliqué
3×5" rectangle of solid green for leaf appliqués
3" square of pink print No. 2 for flower appliqué
18×22" piece (fat quarter) of green print for border and backing
10" square of muslin
10" square of thin batting
Polyester fiberfill
⅛"-diameter black button
Embroidery floss: black

Finished pillow: 9" square

Quantities specified for 44/45"-wide, 100% cotton fabrics. All measurements include a ¼" seam allowance. Sew with right sides together unless otherwise stated.

Cut and Assemble the Pillow

From pink print No. 1, cut:
■ 1 of Pattern A
From solid green, cut:
■ 2 of Pattern B
From green print, cut:
■ 2—2½×9½" border strips
■ 2—2½×5½" border strips
■ 1—9½" square for pillow back
From pink print No. 2, cut:
■ 1 of Pattern C

1. Using the black embroidery floss and a blanket stitch, appliqué the pink print No. 1 basket shape to the light pink print 5½" square.

2. Sew the green print 2½×5½" border strips to opposite edges of the appliquéd basket block. Press the seam allowances toward the border.

3. Add the green print 2½×9½" border strips to the remaining edges of the appliquéd basket block to make the pillow top. Press the seam allowances toward the border.

4. Layer the pillow top, batting, and muslin according to the instructions in Quilting Basics, which begins on *page 113*. Quilt as desired.

5. Thread a needle with pink thread; tie a heavy knot at one end. Take running stitches (approximately four stitches per inch) all the way around the pink print No. 2 C circle, ⅛" away from the edge (see Yo-Yo Diagram). Don't

Yo-Yo Diagram

make your stitches too small or too far away from the edge, or you won't be able to gather the fabric smoothly.

6. Pull the thread, gathering the edge to the center with the wrong side of the fabric hidden inside, to make a small circle or yo-yo.

7. Sew together the solid green B pieces, leaving a ½" opening for turning. Turn right side out. Slip-stitch the opening closed to make the leaf piece.

8. Layer the black button and pink yo-yo atop the solid green leaf piece; sew together. Attach the flower and leaf to the pink basket.

9. Sew together the quilted pillow top and green print backing piece, leaving a small opening for turning.

10. Turn the pillow right side out and stuff with polyester fiberfill. Sew the opening closed. ■

Lynette JENSEN

Lynette Jensen artfully mingles prints and plaids with stripes and florals, a style reminiscent of days gone by. Her choices of colors and fabrics result in designs with a warm, inviting glow. "Heart Blossom Surround," *opposite*, bursts with flavor in Lynette's colors; the same design takes on a Valentine theme in the sample block, *left*.

"In 1975, I became aware of quilting as a heritage craft."

—Lynette Jensen

Lynette Jensen burst onto the quilting scene in 1989 with classic country patterns in rich traditional colors. But it was years earlier, making Christmas quilts for her two tots in 1975, that she became a quilter. She embroidered gingerbread men on 6" squares, and set them amid strips of old-fashioned calicos she found at a general store.

"Many years later, I found out that I was using the Courthouse Steps approach to the Log Cabin," she says. It was the first of many times that her instincts helped her open a door to quilting's past.

"Quilting in 12" blocks combined everything I love."

—Lynette Jensen

Lynette's love of the art was intensified six months after that holiday flurry, at an antique quilt show.

"I was absolutely floored by what I saw," Lynette says of the quilts. "[They were] beautiful." So beautiful, in fact, that they inspired Lynette to begin piecing.

At the show, she was given patterns for 25 traditional quilt blocks. She pieced all of those blocks in less than two weeks, sowing the first seeds of her distinctive look.

"My goal is to create heirloom products with faster techniques."

—Lynette Jensen

Lynette came across the word "thimbleberries" in a magazine many years before she started quilting.

She clipped the word out, "... and tucked it away for a time when I would be doing exactly what I am doing now," Lynette says. "To me, the word represents 'the fruits of the labor of the thimble.' It seems a fitting name for a company that revolves around stitching."

And now, for quilters, Thimbleberries and Lynette Jensen are almost synonymous.

HEART BLOSSOM SURROUND

Materials

1⅞ yards of dark red print for blocks, inner border, pieced border, and binding

¼ yard of gold print for blocks

1 yard of beige print for blocks and pieced border

1½ yards of dark green print for blocks and pieced border

1½ yards of green print for blocks and pieced border

3¼ yards of large floral print for setting squares, setting triangles, corner triangles, and outer border

6 yards of backing fabric

74×97" of quilt batting

Finished quilt top: 69×91½"
Finished block: 8" square

Quantities specified for 44/45"-wide, 100% cotton fabrics. All measurements include a ¼" seam allowance. Sew with right sides together unless otherwise stated.

Cut the Fabrics

To make the best use of your fabrics, cut the pieces in the order that follows.

From dark red print, cut:
- 9—2½×42" binding strips
- 4—1¾×42" strips for inner border
- 3—1⅝×42" strips for inner border
- 24—3½" squares
- 48—2½×3½" rectangles
- 4—5½" squares for pieced border

From gold print, cut:
- 24—2½" squares

From beige print, cut:
- 254—2" squares
- 96—1¼" squares

From dark green print, cut:
- 3—2×42" strips
- 128—2×5½" rectangles

From green print, cut:
- 3—2×42" strips
- 126—2×5½" rectangles

From large floral print, cut:
- 8—6×42" strips for outer borders
- 15—8½" squares for setting squares
- 4—13" squares, cutting each diagonally twice in an X to make a total of 16 setting triangles
- 2—7" squares, cutting each in half diagonally to make a total of 4 corner triangles

Assemble the Units

Heart Blossom Units

1. For one unit you'll need two dark red print 2½×3½" rectangles, one dark red print 3½" square, four beige print 1¼" squares, and one gold print 2½" square.

2. Draw a diagonal line on the wrong side of the four beige print squares. Place two beige print squares on the top two corners of each dark red print rectangle (see

Diagram 1). Stitch on the drawn diagonal lines; trim the seam allowances to ¼" and press them toward the red print pieces.

Diagram 1

3. Add the gold print square to the left-hand side of a Step 2 dark red print rectangle (see Diagram 2). Press the seam allowance toward the gold print square.

Diagram 2

4. Sew the dark red print square to the bottom edge of the remaining Step 2 dark red print rectangle (see Diagram 3). Press the seam allowance toward the dark red print square.

Diagram 3

5. Referring to Diagram 4 for placement, sew together the pieces from steps 3 and 4 to make a heart blossom unit; press. The pieced heart blossom unit should measure 5½" square, including the seam allowances.

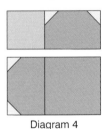

Diagram 4

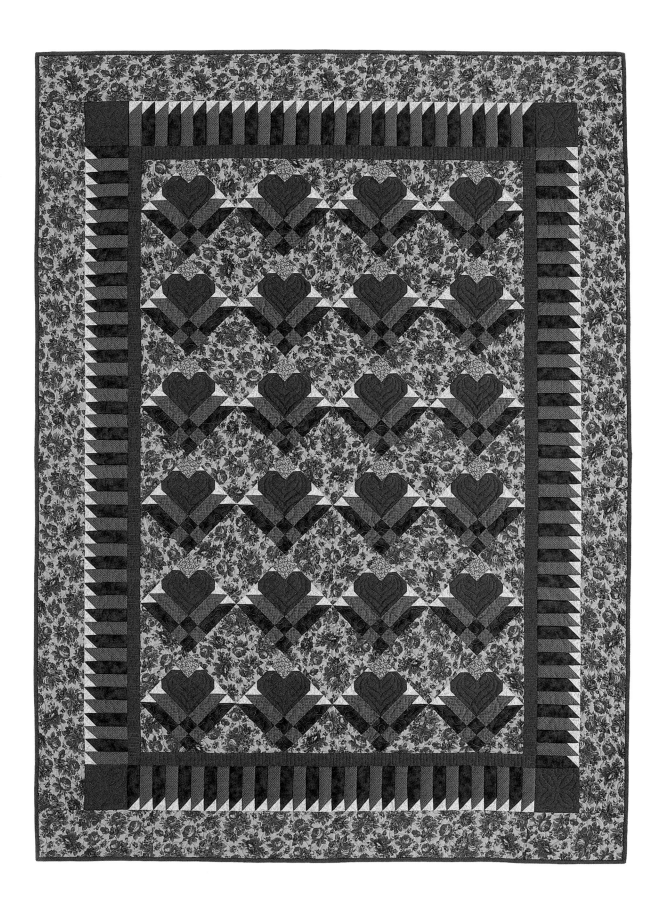

HEART BLOSSOM SURROUND

6. Repeat steps 1 through 5 to make a total of 24 heart blossom units.

Four-Patch Units

1. Aligning long raw edges, sew together one dark green print 2×42″ strip and one green print 2×42″ strip (see Diagram 5) to make a strip set. Press the seam allowance toward the dark green print strip. Repeat to make a total of three strip sets. From the strip sets, cut a total of forty-eight 2″-wide segments.

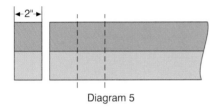

Diagram 5

2. Sew together two 2″-wide segments to make a Four-Patch unit (see Diagram 6). Press the seam allowance in one direction. The pieced Four-Patch unit should measure 3½″ square, including the seam allowances. Repeat to make a total of 24 Four-Patch units.

Diagram 6

Leaf Units

1. Draw a diagonal line on the wrong side of 96 beige print 2″ squares.

2. Place one marked beige print 2″ square on the right-hand end of a dark green print 2×5½″ rectangle (see Diagram 7).

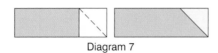

Diagram 7

3. Stitch on the drawn diagonal line to make a right-hand leaf piece. Trim the seam allowance to ¼″; press the seam allowance toward the beige print triangle. Repeat to make a total of 24 right-hand leaf pieces.

4. Substituting a green print 2×5½″ rectangle for the dark green print rectangle, repeat to make an additional 24 right-hand leaf pieces.

5. Sew together the dark green right-hand leaf pieces and the green right-hand leaf pieces to make 24 right-hand leaf units (see Diagram 8). Press the seam allowances toward the dark green leaf pieces. The right-hand leaf unit should measure 3½×5½″, including the seam allowances.

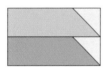

Diagram 8

6. Place one beige print 2″ square on the left-hand end of a dark green print 2×5½″ rectangle (see Diagram 9). Stitch on the drawn diagonal line to make a left-hand leaf piece. Repeat to make a total of 24 left-hand leaf pieces.

Diagram 9

7. Substituting a green print 2×5½″ rectangle for the dark green print rectangle, repeat for an additional 24 left-hand leaf pieces.

8. Sew together the dark green left-hand leaf pieces and the green left-hand leaf pieces to make 24 left-hand leaf units (see Diagram 10). Press the seam allowances toward the dark green leaf pieces. The left-hand leaf unit should measure 3½×5½″, including the seam allowances.

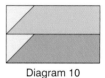

Diagram 10

Assemble the Heart Blossom Blocks

1. Referring to Diagram 11 for placement, lay out one heart blossom unit, one Four-Patch unit, one right-hand leaf unit, and one left-hand leaf unit in pairs.

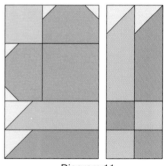

Diagram 11

2. Sew together the pairs. Press the seam allowances toward the leaf units. Then join the pairs to make a heart blossom block. Press the seam allowances in one direction. The pieced heart blossom block should measure 8½″ square, including the seam allowances.

3. Repeat steps 1 and 2 to make a total of 24 heart blossom blocks.

Assemble the Quilt Center

1. Referring to the photograph on *page 35* for placement, lay out the 24 heart blossom blocks, the 15 large floral print 8½" setting squares, and the 16 large floral print setting triangles in diagonal rows.

2. Sew together the pieces in each diagonal row. Press the seam allowances in each row toward the setting squares and triangles. Then join the rows. Press the seam allowances in one direction.

3. Add the four large floral print corner triangles to complete the quilt center. Press the seam allowances toward the corner triangles. The pieced quilt center should measure 46×68¾", including the seam allowances.

Add the Inner Border

1. Cut and piece the dark red print 1¾×42" strips to make the following:
- 2—1¾×71⅛" border strips

2. Cut and piece the dark red print 1⅝×42" strips to make the following:
- 2—1⅝×46" border strips

3. Sew the short dark red print border strips to the top and bottom edges of the pieced quilt center. Then join the long dark red print border strips to the side edges of the pieced quilt center. Press the seam allowances toward the dark red print border.

Assemble and Add the Pieced Border

1. Draw a diagonal line on the wrong side of the remaining 158 beige print 2" squares.

2. Place one beige print 2" square on one end of a dark green print 2×5½" rectangle (see Diagram 7). Stitch on the drawn diagonal line to make a pieced border unit. Repeat for a total of 80 pieced border units.

3. Substituting a green print 2×5½" rectangle for the dark green print rectangle, repeat to make an additional 78 pieced border units.

4. Sew together 16 dark green print and 16 green print border units in a horizontal row (refer to the photograph on *page 35* for placement) to make a short pieced border strip. Press the seam allowances toward the left-hand end of the border strip. Repeat to make a second short pieced border strip. The short pieced border strip should measure 5½×48½", including the seam allowances.

5. Sew the short pieced border strips to the top and bottom edges of the pieced quilt center. Press the seam allowances toward the dark red border.

6. Sew together 24 dark green and 23 green border units in a vertical row to make a long pieced border strip. Press the seam allowances toward the bottom of the border strip. Repeat to make a second long pieced border strip.

7. Add a dark red print 5½" square to each end of the long pieced border strips. Press the seam allowances toward the dark red print squares. Then sew the long pieced border strips to the side edges of the pieced quilt center. Press the seam

allowances toward the dark red border. The long pieced border strip should measure 5½×81", including the seam allowances.

Add the Outer Border

1. Cut and piece the large floral print 6×42" strips to measure the following:
- 2—6×92" border strips
- 2—6×58½" border strips

2. Sew the short large floral print border strips to the top and bottom edges of the pieced quilt top. Join the long large floral print border strips to the side edges of the pieced quilt center to create the quilt top. Press the seam allowances toward the large floral print border.

Complete the Quilt

1. Layer the quilt top, batting, and backing according to the instructions in Quilting Basics, which begins on *page 113*.

2. Quilt as desired. This project was machine-quilted in an allover, meandering pattern.

3. Use the dark red print 2½×42" strips to bind the quilt according to the instructions in Quilting Basics. ∎

Tess HERLAN

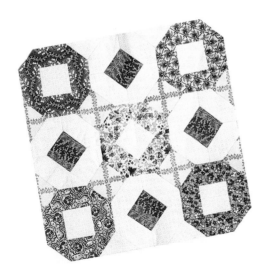

Happenstance started Tess Herlan's foray into English paper piecing. Her "Garden Lattice," *opposite*, is perfect for this assembly method that uses paper templates to join small fabric pieces. Use your favorite scraps and go for a burst of color, as Tess did, or use a simpler palette, as in the sample block, *left*.

"I like to make baby quilts, charity quilts, scrap quilts ... quilts that will cover my grandsons."

—Tess Herlan

Tess Herlan's affection for traditional quilts does not dampen her love of art quilts or her enthusiasm for the tremendous creativity of contemporary quilters. Indeed, from a professional standpoint, she has learned to appreciate other designs and enjoys working with them.

But as for her personal taste in quilts, "I prefer the old-fashioned, traditional patterns," she says.

A gift prompted Tess to try English paper piecing. An aunt gave her some cutaways from a T-shirt manufacturer and she couldn't figure out how to use the stretchy fabric in a quilt.

"I like the accuracy of paper piecing."

—Tess Herlan

"I tried everything to piece that fabric," she says. After much experimentation, she remembered seeing paper piecing in an old book and decided to try it with the T-shirt fabric. "I cut out diamonds, and made a baby block quilt," she says. "It didn't stretch."

Once she found perfection in English paper piecing, Tess had one goal: To inspire quilters to combine pieces with this old piecing method. While she knew English paper piecing went far beyond Grandmother's Flower Garden or Dresden Plate, she had no idea how far. Decades later, after founding, successfully operating, and then selling a paper-piecing pattern business, Tess still has not discovered the full potential of this fine art.

"Quilting is full of endless opportunities for trying something new." —Tess Herlan

"I have a file so thick," she says, "filled with stitches and ideas that have not yet been tapped...." And that pleases her. Because though Tess is retired, she is clear on one thing: "I don't want to get away from quilting."

GARDEN LATTICE

Materials

12—9×22" pieces (fat eighths) of
  assorted 1930s reproduction prints
  for blocks
1 yard of solid white for blocks
  and binding
34×44" of backing fabric
34×44" of quilt batting

Finished quilt top: 29¼×39"

Quantities specified for 44/45"-wide,
100% cotton fabrics. All measurements
include a ¼" seam allowance. Sew
with right sides together unless
otherwise stated.

Make the Templates

You'll need paper templates, one for each
piece in the quilt, unless you want to use a
template more than once.

To make paper templates, trace patterns
A, B, and C onto firm paper the number of
times indicated *below*; cut out. The patterns
are on *page 129.* To make templates from the
patterns, follow the instructions in
Quilting Basics, which begins on *page 113.*

You'll need:
- 192 of Pattern A
- 83 of Pattern B
- 28 of Pattern C

Cut and Prepare the Fabrics

1. Place a paper template on the wrong
side of the fabric. Using the template as a
guide and adding a ¼″ seam allowance, cut
out a fabric shape. (Your seam allowance
does not have to be exact because the
template will be an accurate guide.) Repeat
until you have cut the number specified.

*From each of the assorted 1930s reproduction
prints, cut:*
- 16 of Pattern A
From solid white, cut:
- 83 of Pattern B
- 28 of Pattern C

2. Along one edge of a hexagon, fold the
¼″ seam allowance over the template (see
Diagram 1). Baste in place using a single

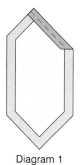

Diagram 1

strand of contrasting thread in a No. 5 or 7
needle, stitching through the fabric and the
paper. Finger-press the basted edge.

3. Fold the seam allowance of an adjacent
edge over the template; baste and finger-
press as before (see Diagram 2). Repeat
folding, basting, and pressing along the
remaining raw edges.

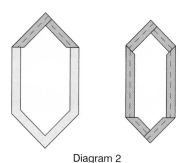

Diagram 2

4. Repeat steps 2 and 3 with the remaining
hexagons, squares, and triangles.

Assemble the Blocks

Use the English paper-piecing technique to
assemble the basted pieces into Kansas
Dugout blocks.

To paper-piece, place two basted pieces
with right (fabric) sides together.
Whipstitch through a pair of folded edges
using a double strand of sewing thread or a
single strand of quilting thread (see
Diagram 3). Designer Tess Herlan likes to
use a quilting needle for this step. You'll be
able to feel the paper templates with your
needle, but do not stitch through them.
Lightly press open the joined pieces.

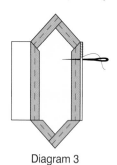

Diagram 3

When paper-piecing, the quiltmaker decides the order of construction because the paper stabilizes the fabric, making it possible to work in any direction. Specific instructions for this quilt follow.

1. Select four basted elongated hexagons of the same fabric and one basted solid white B square.

2. Whipstitch a hexagon to each side of the white square. Then stitch together the angled edges of the hexagons to make a Kansas Dugout block (see Diagram 4).

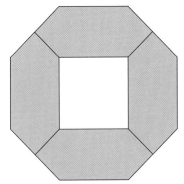

Diagram 4

3. Repeat steps 1 and 2 to make four Kansas Dugout blocks in each of the 12 fabrics for a total of 48.

Assemble the Quilt Center

1. Referring to the Quilt Assembly Diagram for placement, lay out the 48 Kansas Dugout blocks, the 28 basted solid white C triangles, and the remaining basted solid white B squares in eight horizontal rows.

2. Sew together the pieces in each row. Then join the rows; press lightly.

3. Remove the paper templates from all pieces, pulling the basting threads and templates out from the back.

4. Square up the four corners, being sure to leave a ¼″ seam allowance, to complete the quilt top.

Quilt Assembly Diagram

Complete the Quilt
From solid white, cut:
■ 4—2½×42″ binding strips

1. Layer the quilt top, batting, and backing fabric according to the instructions in Quilting Basics, which begins on *page 113*.

2. Quilt as desired. Tess quilted through the center of each of the elongated hexagons in her quilt.

3. Use the solid white 2½×42″ strips to bind the quilt according to the instructions in Quilting Basics. ■

Possibilities

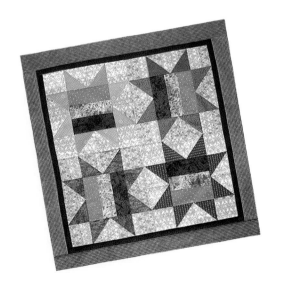

Memory quilts are a favorite of Lynda Milligan, *far left*, and Nancy Smith, the creative forces behind Possibilities. Personal handwriting, memorable verses, and photos transferred to fabric combine to make "Homespun Memories," *opposite*, an heirloom project. Whether you use cozy plaids or colorful prints, you'll inspire reminiscing.

"This is a talent that you can use to give to others."
—Nancy Smith

Lynda Milligan and Nancy Smith became friends in 1977, when they met in a quilt shop. Discovering they had similar interests and complementary talents, they conspired to satisfy a mutual dream, owning their own quilt shop. Four years later, they did just that, opening the Great American Quilt Factory in Denver.

"Quilting is a lifelong passion."
—Lynda Milligan

In their quest to share quilting with as many people as possible, Lynda and Nancy have expanded their skills to include authoring books, designing fabrics, and creating innovative projects for quilters of all skill levels.

Still, they remain focused on what they consider the most important aspect of the business: sharing this heirloom tradition via their shop.

"Quilting is something I grew up with; it's a lifelong passion," Lynda says. "To pass that on to somebody, to watch their eyes sparkle, that's a great feeling."

Projects from quilters both locally and nationally known provide creative sparks for Great American Quilt Factory customers.

HOMESPUN MEMORIES

Materials
⅓ yard of muslin for blocks
1½ yards total of assorted dark prints
   for blocks
1⅝ yards total of assorted light prints
   for backgrounds
1 yard of blue plaid for border
½ yard of blue check for binding
3⅛ yards of backing fabric
56×64" of quilt batting
16×18" piece of freezer paper
Black marker with a wide tip
Permanent black or brown marking
   pen with fine point

Finished quilt top: 50×58"
Finished block: 8" square

Quantities specified for 44/45"-wide,
100% cotton fabrics. All measurements
include a ¼" seam allowance. Sew
with right sides together unless
otherwise stated.

Select the Fabrics

Nancy Smith and Lynda Milligan chose homespun fabrics in plaids and stripes to use in this memory quilt. They incorporated a mix of black, brown, gold, and purple fabrics, making the quilt look warm and inviting. This design lends itself to a block exchange and comes together as a wonderful remembrance to give to a friend. An alternative would be to add words of wisdom to the signature strip.

Cut the Fabrics

To make the best use of your fabrics, cut the pieces in the order that follows.

From muslin, cut:
- 30—1¾×4½" rectangles

From assorted dark prints, cut:
- 120—2⅞" squares, cutting each in half diagonally for a total of 240 triangles
- 60—1⅞×4½" rectangles

From assorted light prints, cut:
- 120—2⅞" squares, cutting each in half diagonally for a total of 240 triangles
- 120—2½" squares

From blue plaid, cut:
- 5—5½×42" strips for border

From blue check, cut:
- 6—2½×42" binding strips

Assemble the Blocks

1. For one block you'll need one muslin 1¾×4½" rectangle, two dark print 1⅞×4½" rectangles, eight dark print triangles, eight light print triangles, and four light print 2½" squares. For each block, Nancy and Lynda used only one dark print for the star and only one light print for the background.

2. Referring to Diagram 1, sew a dark print 1⅞×4½" rectangle to the top and bottom of the muslin 1¾×4½" rectangle to make the center unit. Press the seam allowances toward the dark print rectangles.

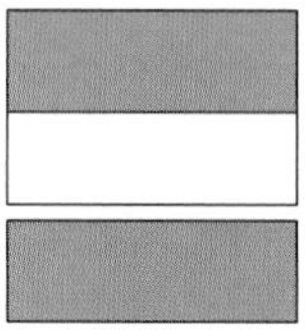

Diagram 1

3. Referring to Diagram 2, sew together a dark print triangle and a light print triangle to make a triangle-square. Press the seam allowance toward the dark print triangle. The pieced triangle-square should measure 2½" square, including the seam allowances. Repeat to make a total of eight triangle-squares.

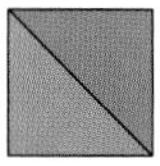

Diagram 2

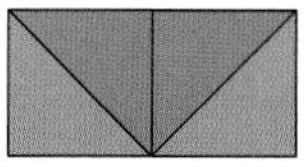

Diagram 3

4. Referring to Diagram 3 for placement, sew together two triangle-squares to make a Flying Geese unit. The pieced Flying Geese unit should measure 2½×4½", including the seam allowances. Repeat to make a total of four Flying Geese units.

5. Referring to Diagram 4, sew a Flying Geese unit to opposite edges of the center unit. Press the seam allowances toward the center unit.

Then add a light print 2½" square to each end of the remaining Flying Geese units. Press the seam allowances toward the squares. Join the units to the remaining edges of the center unit to make a star block (see Diagram 4). Press the seam allowances to one side. The pieced star block should measure 8½" square, including the seam allowances.

6. Repeat steps 1 through 5 to make a total of 30 star blocks.

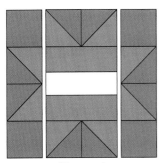

Diagram 4

Sign the Blocks

1. From the freezer paper, cut thirty 2×4″ rectangles. Using a wide-tip black marker, draw a heavy line on the dull side of the paper to act as a placement guide for an autograph.

2. Lay the shiny side of a freezer-paper piece against the wrong side of the muslin rectangle in the center of each star. Iron the paper to the fabric. The black guide line will show through the light fabric. The freezer paper will pull off easily when you have completed your writing.

3. Have friends sign their names on the right side of the muslin rectangle with the permanent fine-point marker. Remove the freezer paper.

For writing on a quilt, select a pen with a fine point that won't bleed as you write. A Sakura Pigma Micron .01 point pen works well because it writes delicately, but the lines it makes can be made thicker by going over them again.

Assemble the Quilt Center

1. Referring to the Quilt Assembly Diagram for placement, lay out the 30 blocks in six horizontal rows.

2. Sew together the blocks in each row. Press the seam allowances in one direction, alternating the direction with each row.

3. Join the rows to make the quilt center. The pieced quilt center should measure 40½×48½″, including the seam allowances.

Add the Borders

1. Cut and piece the blue plaid border strips to make the following:
- 2—5½×58½″ border strips
- 2—5½×40½″ border strips

2. Sew the short border strips to the top and bottom edges of the quilt top. Press the seam allowances toward the outside edges of the quilt center. Sew the long border strips to the side edges of the quilt center to complete the quilt top. Press the seam allowances toward the outside edges of the quilt top.

Complete the Quilt

1. Layer the quilt top, batting, and backing according to the instructions in Quilting Basics, which begins on *page 113*.

2. Quilt as desired. This quilt was machine-quilted in horizontal and vertical lines following the seams in the blocks.

3. Use the blue check 2½×42″ strips to bind the quilt according to the instructions in Quilting Basics. ■

Quilt Assembly Diagram

Helen THORN

Helen Thorn's intricate lodge-look projects most often appeal to experienced quilters desiring a challenge. However, for this wall hanging, *opposite*, she blends tradition and innovation to create a simple seasonal sampler.

"Quilting becomes a passion so easily."

—Helen Thorn

In the late 1980s, shortly after she concluded that hand piecing and hand quilting were not for her, Helen Thorn discovered the rotary cutter.

"And that's all she wrote," she says with a smile. Now she prefers to design using only pieces that can be rotary-cut: squares and rectangles.

In coming up with her designs, she studies photos. "I strive for realism," Helen says.

"Every year it gets better and better."

—Helen Thorn

As of late, she's become addicted to flannel, which works well with her woodsy look and lodge colors—forest greens, earthy browns, deep reds. "Living in Minnesota, I suppose that's understandable," she says of her flannel infatuation.

The variety of notions, fabrics, buttons, and tools available today feeds Helen's imagination, and she is constantly stretching.

"I stray outside my own personal box all the time to work with brights and pastels," Helen says. "Once I make something, I want to try it three, four, 16 different times with different color combinations. I've grown just working with different colors."

SAMPLE THE SEASONS

Materials
2—⅛-yard pieces of light blue prints for blocks
2—⅛-yard pieces of blue prints for blocks
Scraps of assorted prints, stripes, and plaids in red, brown, coral, peach, green, cream, pink, and dark gold for blocks
⅛ yard of rust print for inner border
¼ yard of blue-and-rust print for outer border
⅛ yard of green stripe for sashing
3/8 yard of dark blue print for blocks and binding
¾ yard of backing fabric
29×31" of quilt batting
Assorted buttons

Finished quilt top: 22½×24½"
Finished butterfly, sailboat, snowman, and schoolhouse blocks: 7×8"
Finished leaf, tree, pinwheel, and tulip blocks: 3" square

Quantities specified for 44/45"-wide, 100% cotton fabrics. All measurements include a ¼" seam allowance. Sew with right sides together unless otherwise stated.

Cut the Fabrics
To make the best use of your fabrics, cut the pieces in the order listed in each section.

Piecing Technique
For ease in constructing this wall hanging, incorporate the following steps utilized by designer Helen Thorn.

1. For accurate sewing lines, use a quilting pencil to mark a diagonal line on the wrong side of specified squares. (To prevent your fabric from stretching as you draw the lines, place 220-grit sandpaper under the squares.)

2. When joining pieces that have a drawn diagonal line, sew directly on the drawn line. Cut away the excess fabric, leaving ¼"-wide seam allowances. Press open the attached triangles.

Assemble the Butterfly Block
From light blue print, cut:
- 1—3½" square
- 1—2½×3½" rectangle
- 1—1½×4½" rectangle
- 1—1½×3½" rectangle
- 1—1½×2½" rectangle
- 6—1½" squares

From coral print, cut:
- 2—3½" squares

From peach print, cut:
- 2—2½×3½" rectangles

From cream stripe, cut:
- 4—1½×3½" rectangles

From green plaid, cut:
- 2—1½" squares
- 1—2¼" square

1. Mark a diagonal sewing line on each light blue print 1½" square.

2. Referring to Diagram 1 for placement, align a marked light blue print 1½" square in the upper left corner of a coral print 3½" square. Sew, trim, and press open as described above. Repeat with a second

Diagram 1

marked light blue print 1½" square and the second coral print 3½" square.

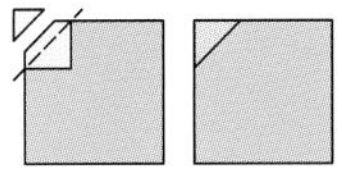

3. Align a marked light blue print 1½" square with one end of a cream stripe 1½×3½" rectangle (see Diagram 2). Sew together, trim, and press as before to make a pieced rectangle. Repeat to make a matching pieced rectangle. Repeat in the same manner, changing the direction of the diagonal line, to make a total of four pieced rectangles.

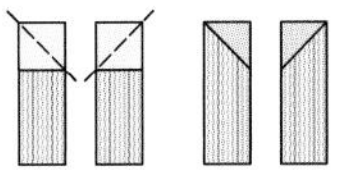

Diagram 2

4. Referring to Diagram 3 and working on the wrong side of a light blue print 2½×3½" rectangle, mark a dot in the upper left corner of the rectangle ¼" from each edge. Mark a second dot in the upper right corner ½" from the right edge and 1¼" from the top edge. Draw a line through the dots.

5. Place the marked light blue print rectangle atop a peach print 2½×3½" rectangle (see Diagram 3). Stitch on the drawn line. With the light blue print rectangle on the bottom, press the peach print rectangle open; trim the assembled piece to the original 2½×3½", including the seam allowances (see Diagram 4).

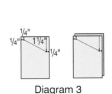

Diagram 3 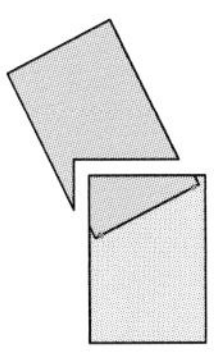   Diagram 4

6. Referring to Diagram 5 and working on the wrong side of the light blue print 2½×3½" rectangle, mark a dot in the lower left corner of the rectangle ¼" from the

bottom edge and 1¼" from the left edge. Draw a line connecting this dot with the original dot made.

7. Place the marked light blue print triangle atop the remaining peach print 2½×3½" rectangle (see Diagram 5). Stitch on the drawn line. Press the peach print rectangle open; trim the assembled piece to the original 2½×3½", including the seam allowances (see Diagram 6).

Diagram 5   Diagram 6

8. With the wrong side inside, fold the green plaid 2¼" square in half to make a rectangle; press. Then fold the rectangle in half again to make a square; press. Aligning raw edges, baste the folded square in one corner of the light blue print 3½" square.

9. Referring to Diagram 7, lay out the pieces for the butterfly block. Sew together the pieces in sections. Then join the sections to make the block; press. The pieced butterfly block should measure 7½×8½", including the seam allowances.

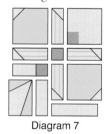

Diagram 7

Assemble the Sailboat Block

From blue print, cut:
- 2—3½" squares
- 1—3½×1" rectangle
- 1—2½×7" rectangle
- 1—2½×4" rectangle
- 1—2½×1½" rectangle
- 1—2½" square
- 2—2" squares

From cream stripe, cut:
- 2—3½" squares
- 1—2½" square

From brown plaid, cut:
- 1—2" square
- 1—¾×7" strip
- 1—¾×3½" strip

From red print, cut:
- 1—2×7½" rectangle

From green print, cut:
- 4—1½×2" rectangles

1. Mark a diagonal sewing line on each blue print 2", 2½", and 3½" square.

2. Referring to Diagram 8, layer a marked blue print 3½" square and a cream stripe 3½" square. Sew on the drawn line. Trim the seam allowance to ¼" and press the triangles open to make a triangle-square. Repeat with the remaining marked blue print 3½" square and the remaining cream stripe 3 ½" square.

Diagram 8

3. Repeat Step 2 using the marked blue print 2½" square and the cream stripe 2½" square to make a blue-and-cream triangle-square. Then repeat using a marked blue print 2" square and the brown plaid 2" square to make a blue-and-brown triangle-square.

4. Mark a sewing line perpendicular to the seam line of the blue-and-brown triangle-square.

5. Align the remaining marked blue print 2" square with one end of the red print 2×7½" rectangle; align the blue-and-brown triangle-square with the other end (see Diagram 9). Sew on the drawn lines; trim and press.

Diagram 9

6. Layer two green print 1½×2" rectangles. Referring to Diagram 10, stitch a triangle. Trim the seam allowances to ⅛". Turn right side out; press to create a flag. Repeat to make a second flag.

Diagram 10

7. With the wrong sides inside, fold the brown plaid ¾×7" and ¾×3½" strips in half lengthwise; press.

8. Referring to Diagram 11 for placement, lay out the pieces for the sailboat block. Sew together the pieces in sections; press. Place the folded brown plaid 7"-long strip along the left side of the two larger triangle-square section; position a flag at the top. Baste the pieces in place. Repeat with the folded brown plaid 3½"-long strip and the small triangle-square section. Position the remaining flag at the top; baste in place.

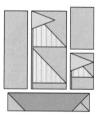

Diagram 11

9. Sew together the sections; press. The pieced sailboat block should measure 7½×8½", including the seam allowances.

Assemble the Schoolhouse Block

From light blue print, cut:
- 2—3" squares
- 2—2×4" rectangles
- 2—2×3" rectangles
- 2—1½×3" rectangles
- 1—1½×2" rectangle

From red stripe, cut:
- 1—3×5½" rectangle
- 2—2½×3" rectangles
- 1—2×3½" rectangle
- 1—1½×1" rectangle

From brown plaid, cut:
- 2—3×4″ rectangles
- 2—1×2″ rectangles

From green plaid, cut:
- 1—1½×2½″ rectangle

1. Place a light blue print 2×4″ rectangle atop the red stripe 2×3½″ rectangle at a right angle (see Diagram 12; note the placement of the diagonal dashed line); sew together, press, and trim. Add the remaining light blue print 2×4″ rectangle to the opposite end; press.

Diagram 12

2. In the same manner, sew a brown plaid 3×4″ rectangle to one end of the red stripe 3×5½″ rectangle (see Diagram 13; note the diagonal dashed line); press and trim. Add the remaining brown plaid 3×4″ rectangle to the opposite end; press.

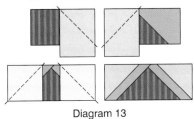

Diagram 13

3. Mark diagonal sewing lines on the light blue print 3″ squares.

4. Align a marked light blue print 3″ square with each end of the pieced brown-and-red rectangle. Sew on the drawn lines. Trim the seam allowances to ¼″; press the triangles open.

5. Referring to Diagram 14, lay out all of the pieces for the schoolhouse block. Sew together the pieces in sections. Then join the sections. Press the seam allowances in one direction. The pieced schoolhouse block should measure 7½×8½″, including the seam allowances.

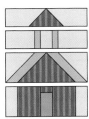

Diagram 14

Assemble the Snowman Block

From dark blue print, cut:
- 3—2″ squares
- 2—2×3″ rectangles

From cream stripe, cut:
- 2—1½″ squares
- 2—1½×2½″ rectangles
- 2—1½×3½″ rectangles
- 4—1½×4½″ rectangles

From brown plaid, cut:
- 1—4½×3″ rectangle
- 1—7½×1″ rectangle

From red plaid, cut:
- 1—1½×7½″ rectangle
- 1—2½″ square

1. Sew together the two cream stripe 1½″ squares along one edge (see Diagram 15) to make the pieced center. Press the seam allowance in one direction. Sew a cream stripe 1½×2½″ rectangle to the top edge of the pieced center (see Diagram 16). Press the seam allowance toward the cream stripe rectangle.

2. Add the remaining cream stripe 1½×2½″ rectangle to the left edge of the block center (see Diagram 17); press.

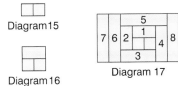

Diagram 15

Diagram 16

Diagram 17

3. Moving in a counterclockwise direction, add pieces to the block center, following the numerical sequence in Diagram 17, to make a Log Cabin block. Always press the seam allowance toward the outside. The pieced Log Cabin block should measure 7½×4½″, including the seam allowances.

4. Sew the red plaid 1½×7½″ rectangle to the bottom edge of the pieced Log Cabin block. Press the seam allowance toward the red plaid rectangle.

5. Mark a diagonal sewing line on each dark blue print 2″ square and the red plaid 2½″ square.

6. Referring to Diagram 18 for placement, align a marked square in each corner of the Log Cabin block. Sew on the drawn lines; trim and press.

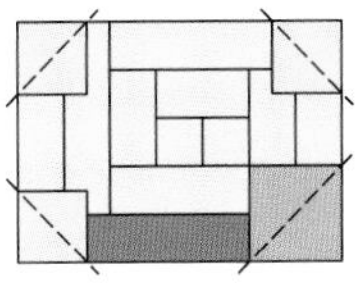

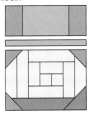

Diagram 18

7. Referring to Diagram 19, lay out all the pieces for the snowman block. Sew together the pieces in sections. Then join the sections to complete the snowman block; press. The pieced snowman block should measure 7½×8½″, including the seam allowances.

Diagram 19

Assemble the Quilt Center

From green stripe, cut:
- 2—2×8½″ rectangles
- 2—2×7½″ rectangles

From dark gold print, cut:
- 1—2″ square
- 8—1¼″ squares

1. Mark a diagonal sewing line on each dark gold print 1¼″ square.

2. Align a marked dark gold print 1¼″ square in one corner of a green stripe 2×7½″ rectangle (see Diagram 20 on *page 56*). Sew on the drawn line; trim and press.

SAMPLE THE SEASONS

Diagram 20

Align a second marked dark gold print 1¼″ square in the adjacent corner of the green stripe rectangle; sew, trim, and press to complete a sashing strip.

3. Repeat Step 2 with the remaining marked dark gold print 1¼″ squares, the remaining green stripe 2×7½″ rectangle, and the two green stripe 2×8½″ rectangles to make a total of four sashing strips. The pieced sashing strips should measure 2×7½″ or 2×8½″, including the seam allowances.

4. Referring to Diagram 21, lay out the four pieced blocks, the four pieced sashing strips, and the dark gold print 2″ square in three horizontal rows. Sew together the pieces in each row. Press the seam allowances toward the sashing strips. Then join the rows to make the quilt center. Press the seam allowances in one direction. The pieced quilt center should measure 16×18″, including the seam allowances.

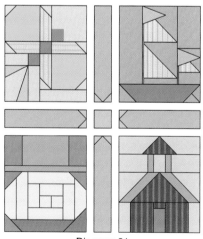

Diagram 21

Cut and Add the Inner Border

From rust print, cut:
- 2—1×18″ inner border strips
- 2—1×17″ inner border strips

Sew the rust print long inner border strips to the side edges of the pieced quilt center. Then add the rust print short inner border strips to the top and bottom edges of the quilt center. Press all seam allowances toward the rust print border.

Cut and Assemble the Outer Border Blocks

Tulip Block

From pink print, cut:
- 2—1½″ squares

From red print, cut:
- 2—1½×3½″ rectangles

From green print, cut:
- 2—2½″ squares

From dark blue print, cut:
- 2—1½″ squares
- 2—1¼″ squares
- 2—1×3½″ rectangles

1. Mark a diagonal sewing line on each green print 2½″ square and dark blue print 1½″ and 1¼″ squares.

2. Layer one marked dark blue print 1½″ square and one pink print 1½″ square. Sew on the drawn line; trim and press to make a blue-and-pink triangle-square (see Diagram 22). Repeat to make a second blue-and-pink triangle-square.

3. Mark a perpendicular sewing line across the seam of each Step 2 blue-and-pink triangle-square.

Diagram 22

Diagram 23

4. Align a marked triangle-square with an end of each red print 1½×3½″ rectangle (see Diagram 23). Note the diagonal

dashed line. Sew on the drawn lines; trim and press to make two flower units.

5. Referring to Diagram 24, sew together the two flower units. Then join a dark blue print 1×3½″ rectangle to each side edge of the flower units.

Diagram 24

6. Align a green print 2½″ square with the lower right corner of the pieced flower unit. Sew on the drawn line; trim and press. Repeat with the remaining green print 2½″ square in the lower left corner.

7. Align the dark blue print 1¼″ squares in the lower corners of the pieced flower unit. Sew on the drawn lines; trim and press to complete the flower block. The pieced flower block should measure 3½″ square, including the seam allowances.

Pinwheel Block

From light blue print, cut:
- 4—2″ squares

From red print, cut:
- 4—2″ squares

From green stripe, cut:
- 4—2″ squares

1. Mark a diagonal sewing line on each red print 2″ square.

2. Layer one light blue print 2″ square and one marked red print 2″ square. Sew on the drawn line; trim and press to make a triangle-square (see Diagram 25). Repeat to make a total of four triangle-squares.

3. Mark a diagonal sewing line on each green stripe 2″ square.

4. Align a marked green stripe square atop each triangle-square, noting that the marked sewing line should be placed perpendicular to the seam line of the triangle-square (see Diagram 25). Sew on the drawn lines; trim and press to make four pinwheel units.

Diagram 25   Diagram 26

5. Sew together four pinwheel units in pairs (see Diagram 26). Press the seam allowances in opposite directions. Then join the pairs to complete the pinwheel block. Press the seam allowances in one direction. The pieced pinwheel block should measure 3½″ square, including the seam allowances.

Leaf Block

From dark blue print, cut:
■ 6—1½″ squares
From pink print, cut:
■ 7—1½″ squares
From brown print, cut:
■ 1—1×2½″ rectangle

1. Mark a diagonal sewing line on four of the dark blue print 1½″ squares.

2. Layer one marked dark blue print 1½″ square and one pink print 1½″ square. Sew on the drawn line; trim and press to make a triangle-square (see Diagram 27). Repeat to make a total of four dark-blue-and-pink triangle-squares.

3. Press under ¼″ along each long edge of the brown print 1×2½″ rectangle. Lay the rectangle diagonally atop a dark blue print 1½″ square (see Diagram 28). Topstitch ⅛″ from the folded edges of the brown strip to make the stem unit.

4. Referring to Diagram 29, lay out the triangle-squares, the stem unit, and the remaining squares in three horizontal rows. Sew together the squares in each row. Press the seam allowances in one direction, alternating the direction with each row.

Then join the rows to complete the leaf block. The leaf block should measure 3½″ square, including the seam allowances.

Diagram 27   Diagram 28   Diagram 29

Tree Block

From light blue print, cut:
■ 2—2″ squares
■ 2—1¼″ squares
■ 2—1¾×1¼″ rectangles
From green print, cut:
■ 1—2×3½″ rectangle
■ 1—1¼×3½″ rectangle
From brown print, cut:
■ 1—1×1¼″ rectangle

1. Mark a diagonal sewing line on each light blue print 2″ and 1¼″ square.

2. Align a marked light blue print 2″ square with one end of a green print 2×3½″ rectangle (see Diagram 30). Sew on the drawn line; trim and press. Add the remaining marked light blue print 2″ square to the opposite end of the green print rectangle in the same manner to make a tree top unit.

Diagram 30

3. Align a marked light blue print 1¼″ square with one end of a green print 1¼×3½″ rectangle (see Diagram 31). Sew on the drawn line; trim and press. Add the remaining marked light blue print 1¼″ square to the opposite end of the green print rectangle in the same manner to make a tree bottom unit.

Diagram 31

4. Sew a light blue 1¾×1¼″ rectangle to either long edge of a brown print 1×1¼″ rectangle to make a tree trunk unit.

5. Referring to Diagram 32, sew together the units to make a tree block. Press the seam allowances in one direction. The pieced tree block should measure 3½″ square, including the seam allowances.

Diagram 32

Cut and Add the Outer Border

From blue-and-rust print, cut:
■ 2—3½×19″ outer border strips
■ 2—3½×17″ outer border strips

1. Sew the blue-and-rust print long outer border strips to the side edges of the quilt center. Press the seam allowances toward the blue-and-rust outer border.

2. Referring to the photograph on *page 51* for placement, sew a pieced outer border block to each end of the blue-and-rust print short outer border strips. Press the seam allowances toward the outer border strips. Then join the pieced border strips to the top and bottom edges of the pieced quilt center to complete the quilt top. Press the seam allowances toward the blue-and-rust outer border.

Complete the Quilt

From dark blue print, cut:
■ 3—2½×42″ binding strips

1. Layer the quilt top, batting, and backing according to the instructions in Quilting Basics, which begins on *page 113*. Quilt as desired.

2. Use the dark blue print 2½×42″ strips to bind the quilt according to the instructions in Quilting Basics. Embellish the quilt with buttons. ■

Piece
O' CAKE

Linda Jenkins, *far left*, and Becky Goldsmith of Piece O' Cake Designs refresh traditional patterns with bright, contemporary colors; their overlay technique simplifies appliqué. The vitality of "An Orchard of Apples," *opposite*, comes, in part, from its many fabrics. In the sample block *left*, the design was set on point.

"Working long distance forced both of us to stretch ourselves a little more."

—Linda Jenkins

"We did clear, bright colors from the beginning," Becky Goldsmith says. Back when only juvenile prints were bright, Linda Jenkins and she were combining clear, brilliant hues with soft, quiet tones.

Now they teach a simplified approach to fabric/color selection and an overlay technique that streamlines the process of appliqué.

"In separate cities, we often buy the same fabric. But we're very different."

—Becky Goldsmith

Their friendship began in the mid-1990s at a Tulsa quilt guild. Amazingly, their business grew when they moved apart.

"Working long distance forced both of us to stretch ourselves a little more," Linda says. More conservative by nature, she brought business savvy to the team, while Becky served as the original idea person. Eight years later, they've grown their own parts of the partnership—and they've each grown more comfortable with the other's end of the business.

With a delightful appliqué style that strikes a balance between primitive and Baltimore, they look forward to designing more fabrics and patterns as they teach quilters through books, seminars, and television appearances.

"Quilters take every opportunity to learn and grow," Linda says. "Their desire to know more and more is growing the industry and keeping it healthy."

AN ORCHARD OF APPLES

Materials
16—13½" squares of assorted light
 prints for backgrounds
16—12" squares of brown prints for
 tree trunk appliqués
Large assortment of scraps in red,
 yellow, purple, and green prints for
 apple and leaf appliqués
⅜ yard of yellow print for border
⅔ yard of red print for border
1¼ yards of purple print for border
 and binding
2 yards of backing fabric
66" square of quilt batting
12" square of clear, upholstery vinyl or
 other flexible plastic

Finished quilt top: 59½" square
Finished block: 12" square

Quantities specified for 44/45"-wide,
100% cotton fabrics. All measurements
include a ¼" seam allowance. Sew
with right sides together unless
otherwise stated.

Select the Fabrics
When choosing fabrics for projects, designers Becky Goldsmith and Linda Jenkins find it helpful to make the obvious choices first. For example, the tree trunks are a significant design element in this quilt, so they started by selecting warm, inviting browns that contrast nicely with the background prints. Then they chose the apple fabrics, but didn't stop with just red. Instead they included colors on both sides of red on the color wheel, ranging from yellow to purple.

Select an Appliqué Method
Becky and Linda have developed their own appliqué method over the years, which uses an overlay for placement purposes. The following instructions are for their overlay method. Your favorite appliqué technique also can be used.

Use the Overlay Appliqué Technique
1. Make templates of the patterns, following the instructions in Quilting Basics, which begins on *page 113*. Mark each template with the proper number or letter to indicate the appliquéing sequence and right sides.

2. Lightly press each assorted light print 13½″ background square in half horizontally, vertically, and diagonally to form placement lines.

3. Cut a 12″ square of clear upholstery vinyl or any other flexible plastic. Center the plastic square over the drawing of the block on the pattern sheet, and accurately trace the entire design, including the dashed placement lines, with a permanent marker (see Photo 1).

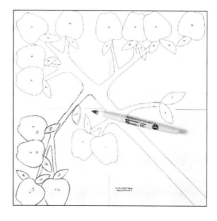

Photo 1

4. Use the templates to cut appliqué pieces, except tree trunks (piece No. 2), from the desired fabrics.

5. Position the overlay on a background square, matching the drawn center lines with the lines pressed in the fabric. Pin the top of the overlay to the fabric, if desired.

6. Slide the first leaf (appliqué piece No. 1) with the right side up between the background fabric and the overlay (see Photo 2). Carefully work the leaf into position. When it is in place, remove the overlay, pin the leaf to the background fabric, and appliqué it in place.

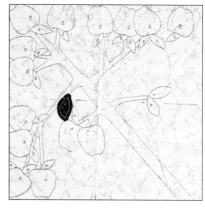

Photo 2

AN ORCHARD OF APPLES

Use the Cutaway Appliqué Technique

To add the tree trunk (appliqué piece No. 2), Becky and Linda used the following cutaway appliqué technique.

1. Lay pattern piece No. 2 atop a brown print square; trace around the pattern (see Photo 3). Do not cut away any excess fabric at this point.

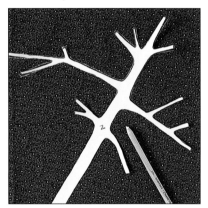

Photo 3

2. Reposition the overlay atop the background square. Slide the brown print square with drawn tree trunk between the background fabric and the overlay, lining up the drawn lines (see Photo 4). The bottom of the tree trunk should extend into the block's seam allowance; it is important to have a full ¼″ seam allowance there. Remove the overlay. Pin or baste the drawn tree trunk in place.

Photo 4

3. Beginning on the left side at the base of the tree trunk, cut away some excess fabric, leaving a scant ¼″ seam allowance (see Photo 5). Begin appliquéing the tree trunk to the background fabric, turning under the seam allowance as you sew (see Photo 6).

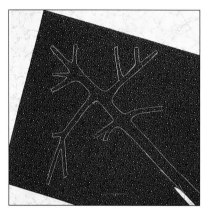

Photo 5

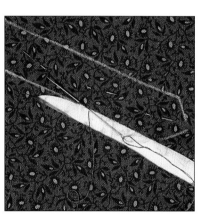

Photo 6

4. Working in small sections, continue cutting away fabric and appliquéing the tree trunk until it is completed (see photos 7 and 8).

Finish the Appliqué

1. Once the first leaf and tree trunk are in place, use the overlay to position the next leaf in the stitching sequence (see Photo 8). Stitch the leaf in place. Working in numerical order, continue in this manner—

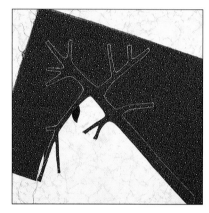

Photo 7

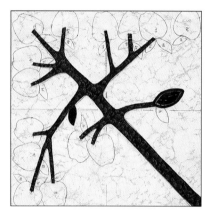

Photo 8

positioning the pieces under the overlay and appliquéing them in place—until the block is completed. Press the appliquéd block from the back.

2. Trim the appliquéd block to 12½″ square, including the seam allowances. Be careful to center the design and to leave the tree trunk extended into the seam allowance.

3. Repeat the appliqué steps to make a total of 16 blocks.

Assemble the Quilt Center

1. Referring to the photograph on *page 63* for placement, sew together four appliquéd blocks in pairs. Then join the pairs to make a four block unit. Press the seam allowances in one direction. The pieced unit should measure 24½″ square, including the seam allowances. Repeat to make a total of four four-block units.

2. Sew together the four four-block units in pairs. Then join the pairs to make the quilt center. Press the seam allowances in one direction. The pieced quilt center should measure 48½″ square, including the seam allowances.

3. Appliqué the bird and nest in the blocks of your choice.

Cut and Add the Borders

The border strips are cut longer than needed to allow for mitering the corners.

From yellow print, cut:
- 8—1½×42″ border strips

From red print, cut:
- 8—2½×42″ border strips

From purple print, cut:
- 8—3¼×42″ border strips
- 7—2½×42″ binding strips

1. Cut and piece the border strips to make the following:
- 4 yellow print 1½×64″ border strips
- 4 red print 2½×64″ border strips
- 4 purple print 3¼×64″ border strips

2. Aligning long raw edges, join one yellow print, one red print, and one purple print strip to make a border strip set. Press the seam allowances toward the purple print strip. Repeat to make a total of four border strip sets.

3. Referring to the instructions in Quilting Basics, which begins on *page 113,* add the border strip sets to the quilt center with mitered corners.

Detail of Bluebird Appliqué

Complete the Quilt

1. Layer the quilt top, batting, and backing according to the instructions in Quilting Basics, which begins on *page 113.*

2. Quilt as desired. Barbara Nimon hand-quilted this quilt all over in a diagonal 1″-wide grid.

3. Use the purple print 2½×42″ strips to bind the quilt according to the instructions in Quilting Basics. ■

Darlene ZIMMERMAN

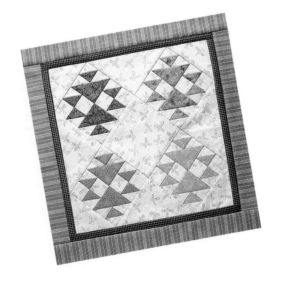

Fascinated with quilt history and an avid collector of vintage quilts and feed-sack fabrics, designer Darlene Zimmerman was inspired by 15 woven plaids to make this wall hanging, *opposite*. She casually combined squares and triangles to create "Butterscotch" from the historic Fox and Geese block. The sample block, *left,* presents a simpler color scheme.

"There is such an incredible variety of fabric, and so many fantastic things people are doing with quilting now ..."

—Darlene Zimmerman

Respect for tradition taught Darlene Zimmerman the importance of an open mind when it comes to quilting.

"Whether you're thinking '30s prints or batik on black, experiment with different layouts," she says. "You get such different looks as you lay a quilt out differently."

"We quilt because we love the process."

—Darlene Zimmerman

One of Darlene's favorite quilts is tied with the strings taken from the feed sacks used to piece the quilt. It was made, most likely, during the '30s, when times were tough. "They didn't waste a thing," she says. "Frugality was a prized virtue."

Darlene has taken this a step further by designing a series of time- and fabric-saving devices for quilters. Her first tool arose out of a desire to help students in a mid-1990s quilting class cut accurate quarter-square triangles.

Just as her tools simplify the cutting of tricky triangles, the reproduction textiles she designs simplify fabric selection.

Vintage designs such as this charming bunny function as focal points in Darlene Zimmerman's quilt and fabric designs.

That's important to Darlene, because it means that more people will get more enjoyment from this heirloom art.

"With quilting, we enjoy the process. The end product is important," she says, "but it is not the only reason we're doing it."

BUTTERSCOTCH

Materials

1 yard of mottled tea-dyed muslin for background

15—⅛-yard pieces of assorted butterscotch, brown, and navy prints, stripes, plaids, and checks for blocks

¼ yard of butterscotch print for borders

¼ yard of brown plaid for binding

24×36" of backing fabric

24×36" of quilt batting

Finished quilt top: 20×32"
Finished block: 4" square

Quantities specified for 44/45"-wide, 100% cotton fabrics. All measurements include a ¼" seam allowance. Sew with right sides together unless otherwise stated.

Cut the Fabrics

To make the best use of your fabrics, cut the pieces in the order that follows.

From tea-dyed muslin, cut:
- 64—1½" squares
- 8—4½" squares
- 123—1⅞" squares, cutting each in half diagonally for a total of 246 small triangles
- 3—6⅞" squares, cutting each diagonally twice in an X for a total of 12 setting triangles
- 2—3¾" squares, cutting each in half diagonally for a total of 4 corner triangles

From each of the 15 butterscotch, brown, and navy prints, stripes, plaids, and checks, cut:
- 1—2⅞" square, cutting it in half diagonally for a total of 2 medium triangles
- 3—1⅞" squares, cutting each in half diagonally for a total of 6 small triangles

From assorted butterscotch, brown, and navy print, stripe, plaid, and check scraps, cut:
- 3—1⅞" squares, cutting each in half diagonally for a total of 6 small triangles

From butterscotch print, cut:
- 2—1⅞×28⅝" strips for border
- 2—1⅞×18½" strips for border

From brown plaid, cut:
- 3—2×42" binding strips

Assemble the Blocks

1. For one block you'll need four muslin 1½" squares, 10 muslin small triangles, six print small triangles, and two print medium triangles. Darlene used the same butterscotch, brown, or navy print fabric in each block, but used 15 different fabrics to make the 15 blocks.

2. Referring to Diagram 1, sew together one muslin small triangle and one print small triangle to make a triangle-square. Press the seam allowance toward the print triangle. Repeat to make a total of six triangle-squares. Each triangle-square should measure 1½" square, including the seam allowances.

Diagram 1

3. Sew together two triangle-squares and two muslin 1½" squares in pairs (see Diagram 2). Press the seam allowances toward the muslin 1½" squares. Then join the pairs to make a Four-Patch unit. Press the seam allowance to one side. The Four-Patch unit should measure 2½" square, including the seam allowances. Repeat to make a total of two Four-Patch units.

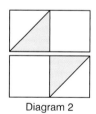

Diagram 2

4. Referring to Diagram 3, sew the short sides of two muslin small triangles to the print sides of a triangle-square. Press the seam allowances toward the muslin small triangles. Then join the long side of a print

Diagram 3

medium triangle to the long sides of the muslin small triangles to make a triangle unit. Press the seam allowance toward the medium triangle. The triangle unit should measure 2½″ square, including the seam allowances. Repeat to make a total of two triangle units.

5. Sew together the two Four-Patch units and the two triangle units in pairs (see Diagram 4). Press the seam allowances toward the triangle units. Then join the pairs to make a block. Press the seam allowance to one side. The pieced block should measure 4½″ square, including the seam allowances.

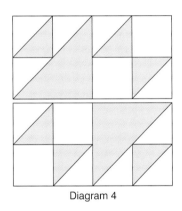

Diagram 4

6. Repeat steps 1 through 5 to make a total of 15 blocks.

Assemble the Quilt Center

1. Referring to the Quilt Assembly Diagram for placement, lay out the 15 pieced blocks, the eight muslin 4½″ squares, and the 12 muslin setting triangles in diagonal rows.

2. Join the pieces in each diagonal row. Press the seam allowances toward the

muslin 4½″ squares. Then sew together the rows. Press the seam allowances in one direction.

3. Add the four muslin corner triangles to complete the quilt center. Press the seam allowances toward the corner triangles. The pieced quilt center should measure 17⅜×28⅝″, including the seam allowances.

Add the Borders

1. Sew the butterscotch print 1¹⁄₁₆×28⅝″ border strips to the side edges of the quilt top. Press the seam allowances toward the butterscotch print border strips. Then add the butterscotch print 1⅞×18½″ border strips to the top and bottom edges of the quilt center. Press the seam allowances toward the border strips.

2. Sew together the remaining muslin and the 96 butterscotch, brown, and navy print, stripe, plaid, and check small triangles to make a total of 96 triangle-squares (see Diagram 1, *opposite*).

3. Sew together 30 triangle-squares to make a long border strip. Note the placement of the triangles in the photograph on *page 67*. Repeat to make a second long border strip. Add the long border strips to the side edges of the quilt top. Press the seam allowances toward the print border strips.

4. Join 18 triangle-squares in a strip. Then add one muslin 1½″ square to each end of the strip to make a short border strip. Repeat to make a second short border strip. Add the strips to the top and bottom edges of the quilt center to complete the quilt top. Press the seam allowances toward the print border strips.

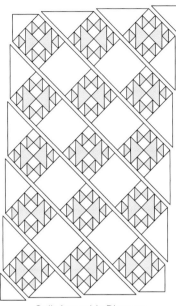

Quilt Assembly Diagram

Complete the Quilt

1. Layer the quilt top, batting, and backing according to the instructions in Quilting Basics, which begins on *page 113*. Quilt as desired.

2. Use the brown plaid 2×42″ strips to bind the quilt according to the instructions in Quilting Basics. ■

Jill REBER

With a style that ranges from contemporary to classic, Jill Reber creates timeless quilts that speak from the heart. In "North Wind Doth Blow," *opposite*, a border of traditional North Wind blocks around traditional Flying Geese, Log Cabin, and tree blocks demonstrates her knack for artful arrangement.

"People are more aware of quilts now, and they treasure them. There are enough easy ways to do things, nobody should be afraid to try."

—Jill Reber

While she doesn't confine herself to a specific style, Jill Reber has a definite favorite. "Traditional. In traditional colors," she says. "I like the old, traditional, pieced blocks."

"What I really like is the geometry— figuring things out."
—Jill Reber

In 1975, when Jill learned to quilt, templates were cut from cardboard. Fifteen years later, still quilting, she asked her husband, Jim Reber, to cut a plastic template. And another. And another.

"He finally said he'd make something that could make all the different sizes, so I wouldn't have to keep interrupting myself," she says. "And he came back with a ruler that is the basis of our rotary-cutting system." The Rebers have since marketed their simplified cutting system to quilters across the continent.

When Jill Reber completed her term as a Des Moines Quilters' Guild officer, guild members presented her with signed Double Nine-Patch blocks. Jill's challenge was to assemble these blocks of assorted colors into an attractive quilt top. Her answer was to combine them with Pinwheel blocks for the quilt *opposite*.

"Quilting is such a productive hobby."
—Jill Reber

In the years since Jill has been designing quilts, she has seen the art form "kind of spread out amongst other people," she says. "Look at any home decorating book or magazine; there is almost always something quilted in the picture."

NORTH WIND DOTH BLOW

Materials

1¼ yards of solid navy for borders and blocks

½ yard of solid gray for borders and blocks

½ yard total of assorted green prints for tree blocks

Scraps of brown prints for tree blocks

½ yard total of assorted burgundy prints for cabin blocks and Flying Geese units

¼ yard total of assorted blue prints for cabin blocks

1 ½ yards total of assorted gray and white solids and prints for blocks

¼ yard of dark gray print for cabins

½ yard of solid burgundy for binding

56" square of backing fabric

56" square of batting

Finished quilt top: 50" square
Finished cabin block: 12" square
Finished North Wind block: 6" square
Finished tree block: 6" square

Quantities specified for 44/45"-wide, 100% cotton fabric. All measurements include a ¼" seam allowance. Sew with right sides together unless otherwise stated.

Cut the Fabrics

Cut the pieces in the order that follows in each section. The patterns are on *page 126*. To make templates from the patterns, follow the instructions in Quilting Basics, which begins on *page 113*.

Assemble the Blocks

Cabin

From solid navy, cut:
- 3—2½×12½" cabin border strips
- 3—2½×10½" cabin border strips

From assorted blue prints, cut:
- 1—2½×3½" rectangle for door
- 4—1½×5½" rectangles for side
- 2—1½×4½" rectangles for front
- 4—1½×3½" rectangles for front
- 4—1½×2½" rectangles for side
- 2 of Pattern B for roof front

From assorted burgundy prints, cut:
- 2—2½×3½" rectangles for door
- 2—1½×5½" rectangles for side
- 1—1½×4½" rectangle for front
- 2—1½×3½" rectangles for front
- 2—1½×2½" rectangles for side
- 6—1¼" squares for chimneys
- 1 of Pattern B for roof front

From assorted gray and white solids and prints, cut:
- 3—3½×1¼" strips for chimney units
- 6—2¾×1¼" strips for chimney units
- 3—2¼×9½" cabin border strips
- 3—1½×10½" cabin border strips
- 18—1½" squares for windows
- 3 *each* of patterns A and A reversed

From dark gray print, cut:
- 3 of Pattern C for roof

1. Referring to Diagram 1 for placement, lay out two burgundy print 1¼" squares, two gray and white solid or print 2¾×1¼" rectangles, and one gray and white solid or print 3½×1¼" rectangle. Join the pieces with the 3½×1¼" rectangle to make a chimney unit. Press the seam allowances toward the burgundy squares.

Diagram 1

2. Referring to Diagram 2 for placement, lay out one each of gray or white solid and print triangle A and A reversed, one blue print triangle B, and one dark gray print piece C. Sew together the pieces to make the roof unit. Press the seam allowances toward the blue and dark gray pieces.

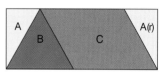

Diagram 2

3. Referring to Diagram 3 for placement, sew together two blue print 1½×3½" rectangles to each long edge of the burgundy print 2½×3½" rectangle. Press the seam allowance toward the burgundy rectangle. Add the blue print 1½×4½" rectangle to the top edge to make the cabin front unit. Press the seam allowances toward the blue rectangle.

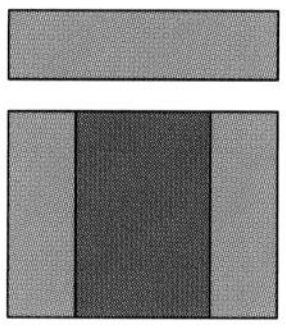

Diagram 3

4. Referring to Diagram 4, sew together six gray or white solid and print 1½" squares. Press the seam allowances in one direction. Add one blue print 1½×2½" rectangle to each end of the pieced squares. Press the

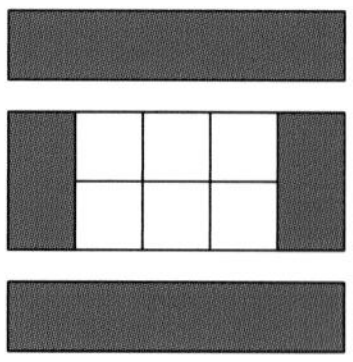

Diagram 4

seam allowances toward the blue rectangles. Then join the blue print 1½×5½" rectangles to the top and bottom of the unit to make the cabin side unit. Press the seam allowance toward the blue rectangles.

5. Referring to Diagram 5 for placement, sew together the cabin front unit to the left-hand side edge of the cabin side unit. Press the seam allowance toward the cabin front unit. Then add the roof unit to the top edge of the cabin front side unit. Press the seam allowance toward the roof unit. Then join the chimney unit to the top edge of the roof unit to make the house unit. Press the seam allowance toward the roof unit.

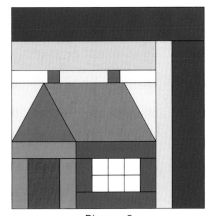

Diagram 5

To the top edge of the house unit, sew a gray or white solid or print 2¼×9½" border strip. Press the seam allowance toward the gray or white strip. To the right-hand edge of the house unit add a gray or white solid or print 1½×10½" border strip. Press the seam allowance toward the gray or white strip. Then join a solid navy 2½×10½" border strip to the right-hand edge of the house and a solid navy 2½×12½" strip to the top edge to make a cabin block. Press all seam allowances toward the solid navy border. The cabin block should measure 12½" square, including the seam allowances.

6. Repeat steps 1 through 5 to make a total of two blue cabins. Then repeat the steps, substituting burgundy print pieces for the blue prints and a blue print for the cabin door, to make a burgundy cabin block.

Trees

From assorted green prints, cut:
■ 10 *each* of patterns E, G, and I
From assorted brown prints, cut:
■ 6—1½" squares for the tree trunks
From assorted gray and white background prints, cut:
■ 10 *each* of patterns D, D reversed, F, F reversed, H, and H reversed
■ 8—1½×6½" rectangles
■ 12—1½×3" rectangles

1. Referring to Diagram 6 for placement, lay out one each of green print pieces E, G, and I and one each of gray or white solid and print pieces D, D reversed, F, F reversed, H, and H reversed in three horizontal rows.

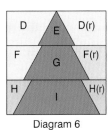

Diagram 6

2. Sew together the pieces in each row. Press the seam allowance toward the gray or white pieces. Then join the rows to make a tree block. Press the seam allowances in one direction. The pieced tree block should measure 6½" square, including the seam allowances.

3. Repeat steps 1 and 2 to make a total of 10 tree blocks.

4. Sew a gray or white solid or print 1½×6½" rectangle to the top of one tree block and to the bottom of a second tree block.

5. Referring to Diagram 7 for placement, sew a gray or white solid or print 1½×3" rectangle to opposite edges of a brown print 1½" square to make a tree-trunk unit. Repeat to make a total of six tree-trunk units.

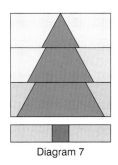

Diagram 7

6. Add the tree-trunk units to the bottom of six tree blocks. Press the seam allowance toward the tree block.

7. Sew a gray or white solid or print 1½×6½" rectangle to the top of three tree blocks with trunks and to the bottom of the remaining three tree blocks with trunks.

Flying Geese

From solid navy, cut:
■ 19—5¼" squares, cutting each diagonally twice in an X for a total of 76 medium triangles
From assorted burgundy prints, cut:
■ 39—2⅞" squares, cutting each in half diagonally for a total of 78 small triangles
From assorted gray and white solids and prints, cut:
■ 37—2⅞" squares, cutting each in half diagonally for a total of 74 small triangles

1. Referring to Diagram 8 for placement, sew one small burgundy print triangle to

Diagram 8

NORTH WIND DOTH BLOW

one side of a solid navy medium triangle, and a gray or white solid or print small triangle to the other side to make a Flying Geese unit. Press the seam allowances toward the small print triangles. The pieced Flying Geese unit should measure 2½×4½″, including the seam allowances.

2. Repeat Step 1 to make a total of 38 Flying Geese units with the background print on the left-hand side of each unit, 36 units with the burgundy print on the left-hand side of each unit, and two units with burgundy prints on both sides.

North Wind

From solid navy, cut:
- 6—4⅞″ squares, cutting each in half diagonally for a total of 12 medium triangles
- 30—2⅞″ squares, cutting each in half diagonally for a total of 60 small triangles

From assorted gray and white solids and prints, cut:
- 30—2⅞″ squares, cutting each in half diagonally for a total of 60 small triangles
- 6—4⅞″ squares, cutting each in half diagonally for a total of 12 medium triangles

1. For one block you'll need one solid navy medium triangle, one gray or white solid or print medium triangle, five gray or white solid or print small triangles, and five solid navy small triangles.

2. Referring to Diagram 9 for placement, join the small triangles to make a unit. Press all seam allowances toward the navy triangles.

3. Add the solid navy medium triangle to one long edge of the Step 2 unit (see Diagram 10). Sew the gray or white solid or print medium triangle to the other

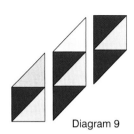

Diagram 9

Diagram 10

side to make a North Wind block. Press the seam allowances toward the medium triangles. The North Wind block should measure 6½″ square, including the seam allowances.

4. Repeat steps 1 through 3 to make a total of 12 North Wind blocks.

Fill-in Units

From assorted gray and white solids and prints, cut:
- 24—2⅞″ squares, cutting each in half diagonally for a total of 48 small triangles
- 24—2½″ squares
- 6—2½×3½″ rectangles

1. Join the remaining 48 gray and white solid and print small triangles to form 24 triangle-squares (see Diagram 11). Press the seam allowances toward the darker triangles.

Diagram 11

2. Join three triangle-squares to make a strip (see Diagram 12). (Note placement of seams.) Press the seam allowances toward

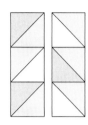

Diagram 12

one end of strip. Repeat to make a total of four strips and four mirror-image strips.

3. Referring to Diagram 13, sew together six gray and white solid and print 2½″ squares in two horizontal rows. Press the seam allowances in opposite directions, then join the rows to make a unit. The unit should measure 4½×6½″, including the seam allowances. Repeat to make a total of four units.

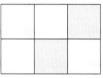

Diagram 13

4. Aligning long edges, join three gray and white solid and print 2½×3½″ rectangles to make a unit (see Diagram 14). Press the seam allowances toward the outside rectangles. The unit should measure 3½×6½″, including the seam allowances. Repeat to make a total of two units.

Diagram 14

Assemble the Quilt Center

1. Referring to the Quilt Assembly Diagram for placement, lay out the blocks, Flying Geese units, and fill-in units in three horizontal rows.

2. Sew together the units in each row. The join the rows to make the quilt center. Press the seam allowances in one direction. The pieced quilt center should measure 36½″ square, including seam allowances.

Add the Borders
From solid navy, cut:
- 4—2½×26½″ strips for outer border
- 2—1½×24½″ strips for inner border
- 2—1½×25½″ strips for inner border

From solid gray, cut:
- 2—1½×13½″ strips for inner border
- 2—1½×12½″ strips for inner border

1. Sew one solid gray 1½×12½″ strip to the end of a solid navy 1½×24½″ strip to make an inner border strip. Press the seam allowance toward the solid navy strip. Repeat to make a total of two inner border strips. Referring to the photograph on *page 73* for placement, join the inner border strips to opposite edges of the quilt center.

2. Sew one solid gray 1½×13½″ strip to the end of a solid navy 1½×25½″ strip to make an inner border strip. Press the seam allowance toward the solid navy strip. Repeat to make a total of two inner border strips. Join the inner borders strips to the remaining edges of the quilt center (see photograph for placement).

3. Lay out two North Wind blocks, 13 Flying Geese units with the burgundy small triangle on the left, and one solid navy 2½×26½″ strip (see photograph for placement). Sew together the pieces to make an outer border strip. Press the seam allowances in one direction. Repeat to make a second outer border strip. Join the outer border strips to opposite edges of the quilt center.

4. Lay out four North Wind blocks, 13 Flying Geese units with the background print small triangle on the left, and one

Quilt Assembly Diagram

solid navy 2½×26½″ strip (see photograph for placement). Sew together the pieces to make an outer border strip. Press the seam allowances in one direction. Repeat to make a second outer border strip. Join the outer border strips to the remaining edges of the quilt center to make the quilt top.

Complete the Quilt
From solid burgundy, cut:
- 6—2½×42″ binding strips

1. Layer the quilt top, batting, and backing according to the instructions in Quilting Basics, which begins on *page 113*.

2. Quilt as desired. Jill machine-quilted in the ditch around each cabin, tree, and Flying Geese unit. Then she added machine-stippling in the background to resemble snowdrifts.

3. Use the solid burgundy 2½×42″ strips to bind the quilt according to the instructions in Quilting Basics. ■

Peggy WALTMAN

For the experienced quilter, Peggy Waltman's designs are an opportunity to use every skill. For the beginner, the same designs provide a chance to learn new techniques. For all quilters, her designs are an opportunity to enjoy learning. "Be Surprised," *opposite*, with its cheerful colors and loving verse, illustrates Peggy's outlook on life.

"This is such a cheerful piece; don't you think that's the object of life?"

—Peggy Waltman

Like a warm ray of sunshine, Peggy Waltman's free-spirited designs cast a cheerful glow. "I like happy colors, I like a crisp look," she says. "I use white or off-white backgrounds because I like to see a clear definition between patchwork and appliqué."

Peggy started quilting to meet her new neighbors after a family move. But it was during a time of poor health that she tackled quilting wholeheartedly. She used her time at rest as an opportunity to learn something new. "I wanted to do my own thing, and this is it," she says.

Those first quilts, made in the early 1990s, were "kind of scary," she says now. She shows them to her students as her own delightful brand of encouragement.

"You don't have to be a perfectionist. Just learn, and enjoy."

—Peggy Waltman

"Each quilt, if you learn one thing that's all that matters," Peggy says. "Go outside the comfortable realm of what you usually pick. Use colors that make you smile."

Some of hers quilts are pieced in bright, vivid colors. Others are embroidered with meaningful verses or appliquéd in exquisite detail. All speak of the delight she takes in this heirloom art.

When she hand-quilts, Peggy often uses contrasting thread. "I want my quilting to show," Peggy says. She also adds French knots for up-close interest.

BE SURPRISED

Materials

8" square of solid white for
embroidery foundation

⅝ yard of green print No. 1 for
embroidery border, dogtooth border,
flower and leaf appliqués, and
binding

9×22" piece (fat eighth) of yellow print
for embroidery border

½ yard of purple print for embroidery
border, flower appliqués, and
outer border

½ yard of white print for appliqué
foundation

⅓ yard of green print No. 2 for flower,
leaf, and stem appliqués

¼ yard of solid yellow for flower
appliqués and inner border

⅛ yard of light green for flower and
leaf appliqués

⅞ yard of backing fabric

31×32" of quilt batting

Embroidery floss: yellow, green,
and purple

Finished quilt top: 26½×28"

Quantities specified for 44/45"-wide,
100% cotton fabrics. All measurements
include a ¼" seam allowance. Sew
with right sides together unless
otherwise stated.

Cut the Fabrics

To make the best use of your fabrics, cut
the pieces in the order that follows.

From green print No. 1, cut:
- 3—2½×42″ binding strips
- 4—1½×24″ strips for dogtooth border
- 2—⅞×10½″ embroidery border strips
- 2—⅞×9¾″ embroidery border strips
- 2—⅞×7¾″ embroidery border strips
- 2—⅞×7″ embroidery border strips

From yellow print, cut:
- 6—⅞×7″ strips

From purple print, cut:
- 3—2½×42″ strips for outer border
- 5—1½×7″ strips
- 2—1½×4″ strips

From white print, cut:
- 2—16″ squares, cutting each in half
  diagonally to make a total of 4 triangles

From green print No. 2, cut:
- 3—1½×42″ strips for inner border
- 4—1¼×11″ bias strips (For specific
  instructions on cutting bias strips, see
  Quilting Basics, which begins on
  page 113.)

From solid yellow, cut:
- 3—1½×42″ strips for inner border

Embroider the Center Block

1. Lightly press the solid white 8″ square
in half horizontally and vertically to
mark the center point; unfold. Center
the fabric on the embroidery design found
on *page 124*, matching the center marks to
ensure the writing will be straight. Note
that the square is placed on point. Use a
quilter's pencil to transfer the verse and
other embroidery lines to the solid white
8″ square.

2. Using two strands of purple embroidery
floss, backstitch the letters and make
French knots for the period and to dot the
i's. Use a backstitch and a French knot to
make each comma.

To backstitch, bring your needle up at A
(see diagram *above right*) and go back down

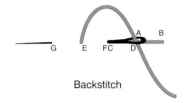

Backstitch

at B. Bring your needle back up at C and
go down at D, pulling the floss taut against
the fabric; continue in the same manner.

To make a French knot, pull the floss
through at A (see diagram *below*), the point
where the knot is desired. Wrap the floss
around the needle two times. Insert the tip
of the needle into the fabric at B, ¹⁄₁₆″ away
from A. Gently push the wraps down the
needle to meet the fabric. Pull the needle
so the floss trails through the knot slowly
and smoothly.

French Knot

3. Using two strands of green embroidery
floss, backstitch the vines and flower
center circles; create the leaves with the
lazy daisy stitch.

To make a lazy daisy stitch, pull your
needle up at A (see diagram *below*), leaving
a loop of floss on the fabric surface. Insert
the needle back into the fabric at B, about
¹⁄₁₆″ away from A. Bring the needle tip out
at C and loop the trailing floss under the
needle tip. Gently pull the needle and

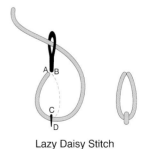

Lazy Daisy Stitch

trailing floss until the loop lies flat against the fabric. Push the needle through to the back at D.

4. Using two strands of purple embroidery floss, satin-stitch the flower petals and fly-stitch the outer edges of the petals.

To satin-stitch, use a quilter's pencil to outline the area you want to cover. Then fill in the area with straight stitches, placing the stitches side by side (see diagram *below*).

Satin Stitch

To fly-stitch, pull your needle up at A (see diagram *below*), form a V shape with the floss, and hold the angle in place with your thumb. Push the needle down at B, come up at C, and push the needle through to the back at D.

Fly Stitch

5. Combine one strand each of yellow and green embroidery floss to make several French knots in the center of each flower. Using two strands of yellow embroidery floss, make a French knot at the tip of each flower petal.

6. Trim the solid white embroidery foundation to 7″ square; press from the back.

Assemble the Quilt Center Block

1. Sew the green print ⅞×7″ embroidery border strips to opposite edges of the embroidered center square. Then add the green print ⅞×7¾″ embroidery border strips to the remaining edges of the embroidered center square. Press the seam allowances toward the border.

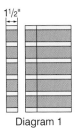

1½″

Diagram 1

BE SURPRISED

2. Aligning long edges, sew together five purple print 1½×7″ strips and six yellow print ⅞×7″ strips, alternating the colors to make a strip set (see Diagram 1). Press the seam allowances in one direction. From this strip set, cut two 1½″-wide segments. Sew the segments to opposite edges of the embroidered center square. Press the seam allowances toward the pieced segments.

3. Join the purple print 1½×4″ strips to each end of the remaining strip set in Step 2 (see Diagram 2). Press the seam allowances in one direction. From this strip set, cut two more 1½″-wide segments. Sew the segments to the remaining edges of the embroidered center square. Press the seam allowances toward the pieced segments.

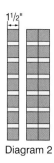

Diagram 2

4. Sew the green print ⅞×9¾″ embroidery border strips to opposite edges of the embroidered center square. Then add the green print ⅞×10½″ embroidery border strips to the remaining edges of the embroidered center square. Press the seam allowances toward the border.

5. Referring to Diagram 3, sew two white print triangles to opposite edges of the embroidered center square, matching center points; press. Fold the center square in half so the triangle points are aligned (see Diagram 4). Trim the sides of the white print triangles even with the edges of the quilt center square.

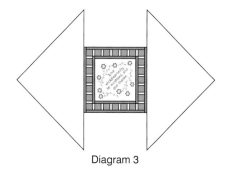

Diagram 3

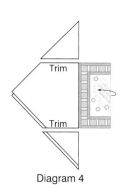

Diagram 4

6. Lay the pieced unit out flat and sew the remaining white print triangles to the remaining edges of the embroidered center square, matching center points to make the quilt center; press. Trim the corner triangles so the quilt center is 21×22½″ (see Diagram 5). This trimming is what allows the dogtooth borders to match at the corners.

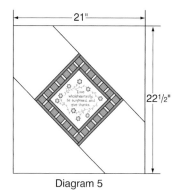

Diagram 5

Appliqué the Stems

1. Fold a green print No. 2 1¼×11″ bias strip in half lengthwise with the wrong side inside. Using a ⅛″ seam allowance, sew together the long edges (see Diagram 6). Roll the strip so the seam is in the middle of one side; press flat to make a stem appliqué. Fold one end ¼″ under at an angle. Repeat to make a total of four stem appliqués.

Diagram 6

2. Referring to the photograph on *page 85*, pin the stems in place on the quilt center. With matching thread, hand-stitch the stems to the quilt center.

Cut the Leaf and Flower Appliqués

Peggy used reverse appliqué to create the flower centers and leaves. In this technique, the upper layer of fabric is turned under to expose the lower layer. The appliqué patterns are on *page 124*. To make templates of pattern A–D, follow the instructions in Quilter's Schoolhouse, which begins on *page 113*.

From green print No. 1, cut:
■ 2 *each* of patterns A and B for leaves
■ 1 of Pattern C for flower center
From green print No. 2, cut:
■ 2 *each* of patterns A and B for leaves
■ 2 of Pattern C for flower centers
From light green, cut:
■ 4 *each* of patterns A and B for leaves
■ 1 of Pattern C for flower center

From purple print, cut:
- 4 of Pattern C for flower centers

From solid yellow, cut:
- 28 of Pattern D for flower petals

Appliqué the Quilt Center

1. Mark the outer sewing lines and vein lines on the green print Nos. 1 and 2 leaves. Cut down the center of each vein line to create the top leaf layers.

2. Cut the light green leaves to the finished size (on the traced lines) to create the bottom leaf layers.

3. Pair each top leaf with a bottom leaf, making sure the right sides of both fabrics are facing up. Appliqué a top leaf to the quilt center, encasing the bottom leaf between the two. Fold under the edges of the vein line, exposing the light green fabric underneath; slip-stitch the edges in place to create the leaf's vein. Repeat with the remaining leaf pairs.

4. Mark the outer sewing lines and cutting lines on the purple print flower centers to create the top flower center layers. Cut the flower centers to the finished size on the traced lines to create the bottom flower center layers. Pair each top flower center with a bottom flower center, making sure the right sides of both fabrics are facing up. Baste the layers together on the dashed line (see Diagram 7). Cut along the solid line in the top layer to make the spiral. Appliqué a top flower center to the quilt center, encasing the bottom flower center between the two. Fold under the edges of the spiral line, exposing the green print underneath; slip-stitch the edges in place to create the two-color flower center. Repeat with the remaining flower center pairs.

Diagram 7

5. Appliqué the solid yellow flower petals around the flower centers.

Prepare and Add the Dogtooth Border

1. Make templates of patterns E and F, found on *page 125,* referring to the Quilting Basics, which begins on *page 113.* Aligning raw edges, trace two of each template onto the right side of the green print 1½×24″ strips. Cut along the pointed edges, adding a ³⁄₁₆″ seam allowance. Turn under each strip's mitered corner seam allowance; baste in place.

2. Align the straight edges of the dogtooth border strips with the raw edges of the quilt center; baste in place. Using matching thread, appliqué the pointed edge of the dogtooth borders in place, hand-stitching the mitered seam lines at each corner.

Add the Borders

1. Cut and piece the solid yellow 1½×42″ strips to make the following:
- 2— 1½×23″ inner border strips
- 2—1½×22½″ inner border strips

2. Sew the short solid yellow inner border strips to the side edges of the pieced quilt center. Then add the long solid yellow inner border strips to the top and bottom edges of the pieced quilt center. Press the seam allowances toward the inner border.

3. Cut and piece the purple print 2½×42″ strips to make the following:
- 2—2½×27″ outer border strips
- 2—2½×24½″ outer border strips

4. Sew the short purple print outer border strips to the side edges of the pieced quilt center. Then add the long purple print outer border strips to the top and bottom edges of the pieced quilt center to complete the quilt top. Press the seam allowances toward the purple print border.

Complete the Quilt

1. Layer the quilt top, batting, and backing according to the instructions in Quilting Basics, which begins on *page 113.*

2. Quilt as desired. Peggy echo-quilted around the flowers and flower petals, filling the remaining white print area and embroidered center square with stipple quilting. The dogtooth border, yellow inner border, and purple outer border were quilted individually with teardrop, circle, and leaf motifs.

3. Use the green print 2½×42″ strips to bind the quilt according to the instructions in Quilting Basics. ■

JOY HOFFMAN

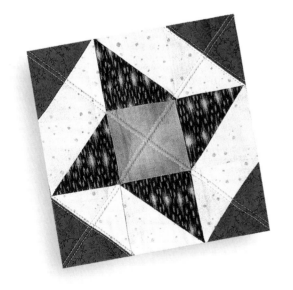

With an engineer-like eye for angles, Joy Hoffman enjoys the geometric challenges that quilting provides. Her "Prairie Stars" quilt, *opposite*, is based on the traditional Nine-Patch block; additional "lines" imprint the piece with depth of field and a sense of movement. The intricate appearance is deceiving; it's easier to assemble than it looks.

"Sometimes you wonder if your choices are brilliant, or just weird."

—Joy Hoffman

Joy Hoffman loves classic color combinations. "And I like to branch off a bit into something that you wouldn't quite put together," she says. "Let the fabric speak to you. Be open to the idea that there is more than one answer, that there is no wrong answer."

Her open mind is evident in her bold use of color and the resulting strong, eye-catching, geometric designs.

"I like quilting on a part-time basis. If I'm busy, I can set the quilting design aside for a while."

—Joy Hoffman

A school nurse, Joy and her husband, Rodney Hoffman, farm 120 miles from Minneapolis. In the late 1990s, they made the switch to organic.

"It's been a good move," she says. "People are becoming increasingly aware of organic farming and are more and more supportive of our efforts."

Joy also develops quilting tools—a sliding stencil, for example—to help people quilt more efficiently, more accurately, and with less frustration.

"Imagine putting a stencil on a quilt. It never comes out right," she says. So she designed stencils with expansion joints that can give or take up to 2". "Fudge space is programmed right in," Joy says. "The stencil expands from and contracts to itself."

PRAIRIE STARS

Materials

3 yards of red leaf print for blocks and outer border

2 yards of off-white print for blocks and middle border

¾ yard of red print for blocks

¾ yard of black print for blocks

2½ yards of gold print for blocks, inner border, and binding

4⅞ yards of backing fabric

74×86" of quilt batting

Finished quilt top: 68×80"
Finished block: 6" square

Quantities specified for 44/45"-wide 100% cotton fabrics. All measurements include a ¼" seam allowance. Sew with right sides together unless otherwise stated.

Cut the Fabrics

To make the best use of your fabrics, cut the pieces in the order that follows. The border strips are cut the length of the fabric (parallel to the selvage).

From red leaf print, cut:
- 2—5½×70½″ outer border strips
- 2—5½×68½″ outer border strips
- 49—6½″ squares

From off-white print, cut:
- 2—1½×68½″ middle border strips
- 2—1½×58½″ middle border strips
- 200—2⅞″ squares, cutting each in half diagonally for a total of 400 triangles

From red print, cut:
- 100—2⅞″ squares, cutting each in half diagonally for a total of 200 triangles

From black print, cut:
- 100—2⅞″ squares, cutting each in half diagonally for a total of 200 triangles

From gold print, cut:
- 2—1½×66½″ inner border strips
- 2—1½×56½″ inner border strips
- 8—2½×42″ binding strips
- 246—2½″ squares

Assemble the Snowball Blocks

1. For accurate sewing lines, use a quilter's pencil to mark a diagonal line on the wrong side of 196 gold print 2½″ squares. (To prevent your fabric from stretching as you draw the lines, place 220-grit sandpaper under the squares.)

2. Aligning raw edges, place a marked gold print square in each corner of a red leaf print 6½″ square (see Diagram 1; note the placement of the drawn lines). Stitch on the drawn lines. Trim on the outside of the stitched seams, leaving a ¼″ seam allowance. Press the seam allowances toward the leaf print square to make a Snowball block (see Diagram 2). The pieced Snowball block should still measure 6½″ square, including the seam allowances.

Diagram 1

Diagram 2

3. Repeat Step 2 to make a total of 49 Snowball blocks.

Assemble the Star Blocks

1. Sew together one red print triangle and one off-white print triangle to make a triangle-square (see Diagram 3). Press the seam allowance toward the red print triangle. The pieced triangle-square should measure 2½″ square, including the seam allowances. Repeat to make a total of 200 red-and-off-white triangle-squares.

2. Sew together one black print triangle and one off-white print triangle to make a triangle-square (see Diagram 4). Press the seam allowance toward the black print triangle. The pieced triangle-square should measure 2½″ square, including the seam allowances. Repeat to make a total of 200 black-and-off-white triangle-squares.

Diagram 3   Diagram 4

3. Referring to Diagram 5, Block A, lay out one gold print 2½″ square, four red-and-off-white triangle-squares, and four black-and-off-white triangle-squares in three horizontal rows.

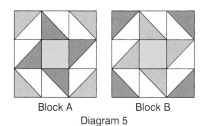

Block A   Block B
Diagram 5

4. Sew together the squares in each row. Press the seam allowances in one direction, alternating the direction with each row. Then join the rows to make a star block A. Pieced star block A should measure 6½″ square, including the seam allowances.

5. Repeat steps 3 and 4 to make a total of 30 of star block A.

6. Referring to Diagram 5, Block B, lay out one gold print 2½″ square, four black-and-off-white triangle-squares, and four red-and-off-white triangle-squares in three horizontal rows.

7. Sew together the squares in each row. Press the seam allowances in one direction, alternating the direction with each row. Then join the rows to make a star block B. Pieced star block B should measure 6½″ square, including the seam allowances.

8. Repeat steps 6 and 7 to make a total of 20 of star block B.

Assemble the Quilt Center

1. Referring to the photograph *above right*, lay out the star blocks and Snowball blocks in 11 horizontal rows.

2. Sew together the blocks in each row. Press the seam allowances toward the Snowball blocks. Then join the rows to complete the quilt center. Press the seam allowances in one direction. The pieced quilt center should measure 54½×66½″, including the seam allowances.

Add the Borders

1. Sew the gold print 1½×66½″ inner border strips to the side edges of the pieced quilt center. Add the gold print 1½×56½″ inner border strips to the top and bottom edges of the pieced quilt center. Press all seam allowances toward the gold print border.

2. Sew the off-white print 1½×68½″ middle border strips to the side edges of the quilt center. Then add the off-white print 1½×58½″ middle border strips to the top and bottom edges of the pieced quilt center. Press all seam allowances toward the off-white print border.

3. Sew the red leaf print 5½×70½″ outer border strips to the side edges of the pieced quilt center. Then add the leaf print 5½×68½″ outer border strips to the top and bottom edges of the pieced quilt center to complete the quilt top.

Complete the Quilt

1. Layer the quilt top, batting, and backing according to the instructions in Quilting Basics, which begins on *page 113*. Quilt as desired.

2. Use the gold print 2½×42″ strips to bind the quilt according to the instructions in Quilting Basics. ∎

Nancy MARTIN

A notable expert on traditional quiltmaking, Nancy J. Martin is the founder and president of a craft and hobby publishing company. She's best known for combining her two favorite subjects, quilting and decorating, in unconventional ways. "Uncle Sam's Salute," *opposite*, is her folksy interpretation of patriotism.

"I love quilting."

—Nancy Martin

She'd always enjoyed crafts. But when she learned to quilt, Nancy J. Martin knew that she had found her creative medium.

"I love very geometric things, and quilting is certainly that," she says. "I like tactile things, and quilting is certainly that. Mainly I like working with color."

Nancy keeps her skills current by creating a colorful quilt in celebration of each Martingale and Company employee's 10th anniversary. "Out of all this quilting and stitching, new ideas emerge," she says.

Nancy has been searching for new ideas since the late 1970s, when she decided to use her teaching background to write quiltmaking instructions. Meanwhile, her husband, Dan Martin, explored the publishing aspects of a quilt venture. Soon they were off and running.

"As the business evolved, we started doing books in a lot of different craft areas," she says. "Enabling other teachers and authors to publish their work is fun—I love the interaction with creative people."

"The water-color quilt movement taught us to look at fabric and design in a different way."

—Nancy Martin

"I feel proud that we were the first to bring out a book on water-color quilts," says Nancy, who was awarded the 2002 Silver Star Award for her contributions to the quilting industry. "From there, we just kept going and in many directions, with new quilting techniques like fusible backing and quick-piece variations."

In quilting these days, Nancy sees an increased interest in working with new materials—wool felt appliqué, for instance, with a versatile motif repeated in pillows and hooked rugs.

"A lot of these projects are small and portable," she says. "Perfect for busy people who enjoy a broad range of creative talents."

Nancy Martin's company extends the art of quilting to include home decor items.

UNCLE SAM'S SALUTE

Materials

⅝ yard of cream print for blocks

Scrap of red-and-cream stripe for blocks

¼ yard of navy print for blocks

Scraps of solid white, peach, and black for blocks

Scraps of red floral, white, dark red, and red prints for blocks

⅜ yard of dark red star print for sashing and inner border

¾ yard of navy anchor print for outer border and binding

1⅓ yards of backing fabric

38×48" of quilt batting

4—11"-tall flags

Finished quilt top: 32×42"

Finished block: 10×15"

Quantities specified for 44/45"-wide, 100% cotton fabrics. All measurements include a ¼" seam allowance. Sew with right sides together unless otherwise stated.

Cut the Fabrics

To make the best use of your fabrics, cut the pieces in the order that follows. The beard pattern is on *page 129*. To make a template of Beard Pattern, follow the instructions in Quilting Basics, which begins on *page 113*.

From cream print, cut:
- 4—4×15½" rectangles for position W
- 4—3½×2½" rectangles for position D
- 4—3½×3" rectangles for position L
- 4—3×9" rectangles for position T
- 4—2½×1" rectangles for position G
- 4—2×2½" rectangles for position A
- 4—2×3" rectangles for position H
- 4—2×1" rectangles for position V
- 4—1½×4½" rectangles for position O
- 4—1" squares for position E

From red-and-cream stripe, cut:
- 4—2½×2" rectangles for position B

From navy print, cut:
- 4—3½" squares for position P
- 4—3×1½" rectangles for position S
- 4—2½×1" rectangles for position C
- 4—1½×5" rectangles for position M

From dark red prints, cut:
- 4—4½×1" rectangles for position F

From solid white, cut:
- 4—¾×3" rectangles for position I
- 4—¾×3" rectangles for position K

From solid peach, cut:
- 4—2×3" rectangles for position J
- 8—1½" squares for position N

From red floral, cut:
- 4—3½×1" rectangles for position Q

From red print, cut:
- 4—3½×6½" rectangles for position R

From solid black, cut:
- 4—5½×1" rectangles for position U

From white print, cut:
- 4 of Beard Pattern

From dark red star print, cut:
- 3—2½×32½" strips for sashing and inner border
- 2—2½×26½" inner border strips
- 2—2½×10½" sashing strips

From navy anchor print, cut:
- 4—2½×42" binding strips
- 2—3½×36½" outer border strips
- 2—3½×32½" outer border strips

Assemble the Uncle Sam Blocks

1. Referring to the Block Assembly Diagram for placement, lay out one each of pieces A through V in sections. Sew together the pieces in each section. Then join the sections to make a rectangle.

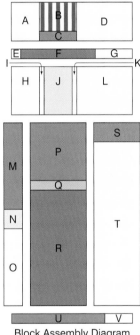

Block Assembly Diagram

2. Fold a solid peach N square in half diagonally. Stitch along one raw edge to create a triangle. Turn right side out. Align the remaining raw edges of the peach triangle with the raw edge of the navy print S rectangle; baste in place.

3. Sew the cream print W rectangle to the right-hand edge of the Uncle Sam rectangle, catching the peach triangle in the seam to make his hand and to complete the Uncle Sam block. The pieced Uncle Sam block should measure 10½×15½", including the seam allowances. Tack the point of the peach triangle to the quilt center to create a loop to hold a flag.

4. Using white thread, appliqué the white print beard piece atop the solid peach J rectangle to create a beard.

5. Repeat steps 1 through 4 to make a total of four Uncle Sam blocks.

Assemble the Quilt Center

1. Referring to the photograph *right,* lay out the four pieced blocks, the two dark red star print 2½×10½" sashing strips, and the three dark red star print 2½×32½" strips in vertical rows. Sew together the blocks and short sashing strips. Press the seam allowances toward the sashing strips. Then sew together the vertical rows to make the quilt center. Press the seam allowances toward the sashing strip and inner border.

2. Add the dark red star print 2½×26½" inner border strips to the top and bottom edges of the quilt center. Press the seam allowances toward the red inner border.

3. Sew the navy anchor print 3½×36½" outer border strips to the side edges of the quilt center. Then join the navy anchor print 3½×32½" outer border strips to the top and bottom edges of the pieced quilt center to complete the quilt top. Press all seam allowances toward the navy outer border.

Complete the Quilt

1. Layer the quilt top, batting, and backing according to the instructions in Quilting Basics, which begins on *page 113.*

2. Quilt as desired. Nancy Martin hand-quilted a radiating fan design in each block,

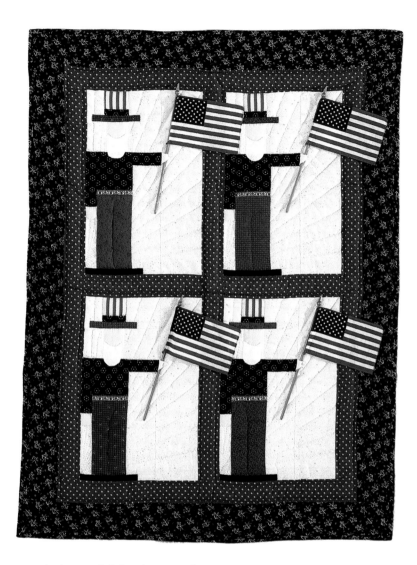

starting in the bottom left-hand corner of each block. She outline quilted the sashing and inner border. In the outer border she hand-quilted a cable design. Nancy also quilted a seam in the center of the red print R rectangles to create "legs."

3. Use the navy anchor print 2½×42" strips to bind the quilt according to the instructions in Quilting Basics.

4. Insert flags in hand loops. ■

Debbie
FIELD

For quilters around the globe, Debbie Field's nature prints and appliqué templates define North Woods style. In "A Walk Through the Pines," *opposite*, her simple color strategy highlights the beloved pine-tree shape against a snowy white background. Debbie's table runner is equally heartwarming in the optional color palette, *left*.

"When your spirit is in something that you truly love, it is natural."

—Debbie Field

Debbie Field's first quilting attempt was a 1987 quilt class. "I loved the piecing, but I wanted to add family artwork," she says. "That's where the appliqué templates came in, and that's what I fell in love with."

Her next challenge was finding fabric she wanted. When she couldn't find anything she liked, she designed it. Her first book, *Making Tracks*, was the basis of that first fabric line.

"A little bit of piecing and our life stories: snowshoes, kayaks, and wildlife."

—Debbie Field

Debbie speaks from the heart with her work, which is filled with reflections of nature—bears foraging, elk grazing, and buffalo roaming.

"When we're cross-country skiing, we see wildlife that other people don't get to see," she says. And so she interprets it in her fabric designs, appliqué templates, and quilt projects. Wildlife blends with acorns and oak leaves in a masculine, North Woods kind of way.

"The log cabins, snowshoes, moose, paw prints, bears—this is my life," Debbie says. "Now that I know this brings so much joy to other people, I'd love to continue the North Woods fabric line.

"It has a calming serenity and just says 'welcome.' I think that's why people are decorating their homes with a North Woods theme. It's a breath of fresh air."

Debbie FIELD

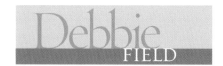

WALK THROUGH THE PINES

Materials

⅓ yard of dark green print for blocks
⅓ yard of green print for blocks
½ yard of light tan print for blocks
¼ yard of dark purple print for inner border
⅞ yard of dark tan print for outer border and binding
1⅜ yards of backing fabric
30×50" of quilt batting

Finished quilt top: 43¼×23"
Finished block: 4¾×13"

Quantities specified for 44/45"-wide, 100% cotton fabrics. All measurements include a ¼" seam allowance. Sew with right sides together unless otherwise stated.

Cut the Fabrics

To make the best use of your fabrics, cut the pieces in the order that follows.

From dark green print, cut:
- 3—2×11⅞" strips
- 21—2½" squares, cutting each in half diagonally for a total of 42 triangles
- 6—1⅞" squares

From green print, cut:
- 4—2×8⅝" rectangles
- 20—2½" squares, cutting each in half diagonally for a total of 40 triangles
- 8—1⅞" squares

From light tan print, cut:
- 4—3¾×5¼" rectangles
- 41—2½" squares, cutting each in half diagonally for a total of 82 triangles
- 14—2⅛×2⅞" rectangles

From dark purple print, cut:
- 2—1½×33¾" inner border strips
- 2—1½×15½" inner border strips

From dark tan print, cut:
- 4—2¾×42" binding strips
- 2—4½×35¾" outer border strips
- 2—4½×23½" outer border strips

Assemble the Blocks

1. Sew together one green print triangle and one light tan print triangle to make a green-and-tan triangle-square (see Diagram 1). Press the seam allowance toward the green print triangle. The triangle-square should measure 2⅛" square, including the seam allowances. Repeat to make a total of 40 green-and-tan triangle-squares.

2. Lay out five green-and-tan triangle-squares in a vertical row (see Diagram 2; note the direction of the diagonal seam lines). Sew together to make the left side of a short tree unit. Press the seam allowances in one direction. In the same manner, but with the diagonal seam lines running in the opposite direction, sew together five green-and-tan triangle-squares to make the right side of a short tree unit. Then join the pieced triangle-square rows to opposite edges of a green print 2×8⅝" rectangle to complete a short pieced tree unit. Press the seam allowances toward the center strip. The short pieced tree unit should measure 5¼×8⅝", including the seam allowances.

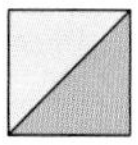

Diagram 1

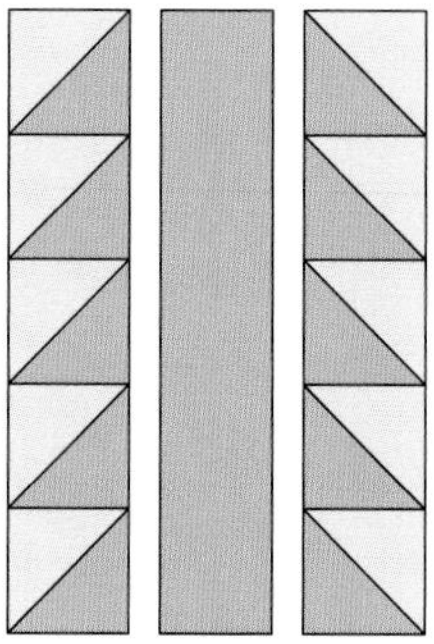

Diagram 2

3. Press two green print 1⅞" squares in half diagonally. Referring to Diagram 3, position a pressed square on the lower right-hand corner of a light tan print 2⅛×2⅞" rectangle; sew across the pressed diagonal line to make half of a treetop unit.

Trim the seam allowance to ¼" and press it toward the green triangle. Repeat, sewing the second pressed square on the lower left-hand corner of the tan print rectangle to make the opposite half of the treetop unit. Then join the two treetop halves to make a treetop unit.

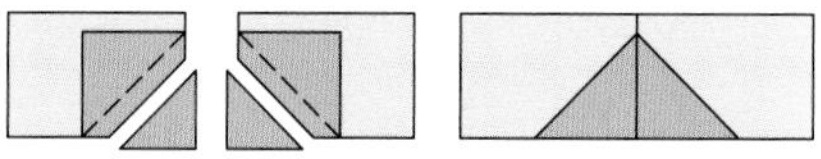

Diagram 3

4. Sew the treetop unit to the top edge of the pieced short tree unit.

5. Repeat steps 2 through 4 to make a total of four pieced short tree blocks.

6. Sew a light tan 3¾×5¼″ rectangle to the top edge of each short tree block. The finished block should measure 5¼×13½″, including the seam allowances.

7. Repeat Step 1 using dark green print triangles and light tan print triangles to make a total of 42 dark-green-and-tan triangle-squares.

8. Repeat Step 2 using seven triangle-squares per side and the dark green print 2×11⅞″ rectangles to make a total of three pieced tall tree units.

9. Repeat steps 3 and 4 using the dark green print 1⅞″ squares and the remaining light tan print 2⅛×2⅞″ rectangles to make a pieced tall tree block. The finished tall tree block should measure 5¼×13½″, including seam allowances. Repeat to make a total of three pieced tall tree blocks.

Assemble the Quilt Center
Referring to the photograph *above* for placement, sew together the pieced tree blocks to make the quilt center. The pieced quilt center should measure 33¾×13½″, including the seam allowances.

Add the Borders
1. Sew the dark purple print 1½×33¾″ inner border strips to the top and bottom edges of the pieced quilt center. Then sew the dark purple print 1½×15½″ inner border strips to the side edges of the pieced quilt center. Press all seam allowances toward the dark purple print inner border.

2. Sew the dark tan print 4½×35¾″ outer border strips to the top and bottom edges of the pieced quilt center. Then sew the dark tan print 4½×23½″ outer border strips to the side edges of the pieced quilt center to complete the quilt top.

Complete the Quilt
1. Layer the quilt top, batting, and backing according to the instructions in Quilting Basics, which begins on *page 113*.

2. Quilt as desired. This project was machine-stippled in the center's light tan areas, quilted in the ditch between the inner and outer borders, and quilted in a meandering design that loosely follows the fabric's leaf pattern on the outer border.

3. Use the dark tan print 2¾×42″ strips to bind the quilt according to the instructions in Quilting Basics. ■

Marti
MICHELL

Marti Michell uses a plethora of prints in a rainbow of colors to create depth and bring out subtle designs. Note, for instance, the illusion of circles in her "Sticks and Stones," *opposite*. Marti designed this quilt using familiar, easy blocks—the three-strip Fence Rail, the Nine-Patch, and a solid square. The sample block, *left,* blends plaids with prints.

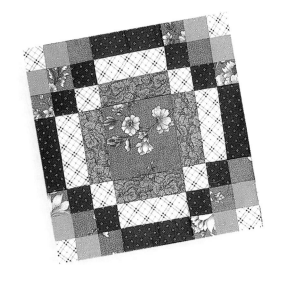

"You can use fewer fabrics, but the more I use, the more fun I have."

—Marti Michell

Marti Michell's use of fabric is a statement of style in itself. As comfortable with hand-dyed batiks as she is vintage prints, a playful attention to detail is Marti's hallmark. Punches of color often reveal unexpected shapes.

"I really like the secondary patterns to keep it interesting," she says. "Such surprising mixes of color can be coordinated successfully."

"Pioneer women had a better selection of cotton fabric than quilters did when we started producing patchwork kits."

There were few quilting resources in 1969, when Marti, then teaching textiles and sewing on the university level, started experimenting with patchwork.

"I had pretty scraps from summer cottons," she says. "I made my daughter a patchwork prairie dress." Her pupils thought it looked like more fun than what they were studying, and asked her to teach them.

Her students loved Marti's color combinations, but finding cottons was "nearly impossible," Marti says. So she began making kits of fabrics she

handpicked. "Before we knew it my husband, Dick [Michell], and I had a patchwork company."

At that time, notions distributors didn't cater to quilt shops' minimal needs for needles, thread, scissors, and thimbles. Quilting books weren't being published.

The Michells' company stepped in, publishing books and distributing supplies that quilt shops couldn't get elsewhere. It helped fuel the groundswell of interest in quilting sparked by the 1976 bicentennial.

Marti's focus today is making quilting easier and more accessible. And now, once again, "people like kits," she says. So she's back to what she loves best: designing quilts, selecting fabrics, and teaching this beloved art.

"That first jump, from not quilting to quilting, is the important one."

—Marti Michell

"The great thing is having such fun all these years," Marti says. "Of course, the key is to have fun."

STICKS AND STONES

Materials
3 yards of black floral for borders
1⅛ yards of black print for blocks
1 yard of red print for blocks
1⅞ yards of tan print for blocks
1⅛ yards of tan floral for blocks
1⅔ yards of green print for blocks
6 yards of backing fabric
88×106" of quilt batting

Finished quilt top: 81¼×99¼"

Quantities specified for 44/45"-wide, 100% cotton fabrics. All measurements include a ¼" seam allowance. Sew with right sides together unless otherwise stated.

Select the Fabrics
The illusion of circles depends on fabric placement and contrast. Select fabrics in four color ranges—dark, medium dark, medium, and light. Use the darkest fabric for the dominant circle pattern, and the medium dark for the less prominent second set of circles. The greater the contrast of these fabrics with the light background, the more the "circles" will stand out. The large solid squares and wide outer border of the quilt can easily handle the scale and drama of a large floral pattern.

Cut the Fabrics
To make the best use of your fabrics, cut the pieces in the order that follows. The black floral border strips are cut lengthwise (parallel to the selvage).

From black floral, cut:
- 2—7¼×86¼" border strips
- 2—7¼×81¾" border strips
- 10—2½×42" binding strips
- 32—5" squares

From black print, cut:
- 12—2×42" strips
- 7—1⅛×42" strips for border

From red print, cut:
- 14—2×42" strips

From tan print, cut:
- 20—2×42" strips
- 7—1¾×42" strips for border

From tan floral, cut:
- 9—2×42" strips
- 31—5" squares

From green print, cut:
- 14—2×42" strips
- 8—3¼×42" strips for border

Assemble the Units
Railfence Unit A
1. Aligning long edges, sew together one red print 2×42" strip, one tan print 2×42" strip, and one green print 2×42" strip to make a strip set (see Diagram 1). Press the seam allowances toward the red and green strips. Repeat to make a total of eight strip sets.

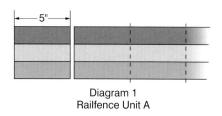

Diagram 1
Railfence Unit A

2. Cut the strip sets into sixty-two 5"-wide segments for Railfence Unit A.

Railfence Unit B
1. Aligning long edges, sew together one black print 2×42" strip, one tan print 2×42" strip, and one green print 2×42" strip to make a strip set (see Diagram 2). Press the seam allowances toward the black and green strips. Repeat to make a total of six strip sets.

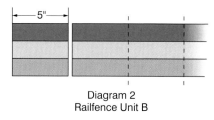

Diagram 2
Railfence Unit B

2. Cut the strip sets into forty-eight 5"-wide segments for Railfence Unit B.

Nine-Patch Unit
1. Aligning long edges, sew together one tan floral 2×42" strip, one red print 2×42" strip, and one tan print 2×42" strip to make strip set A (see Diagram 3). Press the seam allowances toward the red strips. Repeat to make a total of three strip sets.

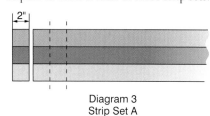

Diagram 3
Strip Set A

2. Cut the strip sets into forty-eight 2″-wide segments.

3. Aligning long edges, sew together one black print 2×42″ strip, one tan floral 2×42″ strip, and one red print 2×42″ strip to make strip set B (see Diagram 4). Press the seam allowance toward the black and red strips. Repeat to make a total of three strip sets.

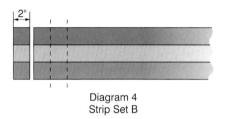

Diagram 4
Strip Set B

4. Cut the strip sets into forty-eight 2″-wide segments.

5. Aligning long edges, sew together one tan print 2×42″ strip, one black print 2×42″ strip, and one tan floral 2×42″ strip to make strip set C (see Diagram 5). Press the seam allowance toward the black strip. Repeat to make a total of three strip sets.

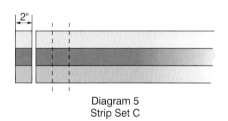

Diagram 5
Strip Set C

6. Cut the strip sets into forty-eight 2″-wide segments.

7. Sew together one Strip Set A segment, one Strip Set B segment, and one Strip Set C segment to make a Nine-Patch unit (see Diagram 6). Press the seam allowances toward the Strip Set B segment. The pieced Nine-Patch unit should measure 5″ square, including the seam allowances. Repeat to make a total of 48 Nine-Patch units.

A B C
Diagram 6
Nine-Patch Unit

Assemble the Blocks

1. Referring to Diagram 7 for placement, lay out four of Railfence Unit A, four of Railfence Unit B, four Nine-Patch Units, two black floral 5″ squares, and two tan floral 5″ squares in four horizontal rows.

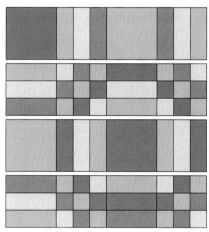

Diagram 7

2. Sew together the pieces in each row. Press the seam allowances toward the Railfence units. Then join the rows to make a block. Press the seam allowances in one direction. The pieced block should measure 18½″ square, including the seam allowances.

3. Repeat steps 1 and 2 to make a total of 12 blocks.

Assemble the Quilt Center

1. Referring to Quilt Assembly Diagram on *page 112* for placement, lay out the blocks in four horizontal rows.

2. Sew together the blocks in each row. Press the seam allowances in one direction,

alternating the direction with each row. Then join the rows. Press the seam allowances in one direction.

3. Referring to the Quilt Assembly Diagram on *page 112* for placement, sew together eight of Railfence Unit A, four black floral 5″ squares, and four tan floral 5″ squares in a row to make a side sashing unit. Then join the side sashing unit to the side edge of the pieced block rows.

4. Sew together six of Railfence Unit A, four black floral 5″ squares, and three tan floral 5″ squares in a row to make a bottom sashing unit. Then join the bottom sashing unit to the bottom edge of the pieced block rows to complete the quilt center. The pieced quilt center should measure 59×77″, including the seam allowances.

Add the Borders

1. Cut and piece the tan print 1¾×42″ strips to make the following:
- 2—1¾×77″ border strips
- 2—1¾×61½″ border strips

2. Sew the long tan print border strips to the side edges of the pieced quilt center. Then join the short tan print border strips to the top and bottom edges of the quilt center. Press all seam allowances toward the tan print border.

3. Cut and piece the black print 1⅛×42″ strips to make the following:
- 2—1⅛×79½″ border strips
- 2—1⅛×62¾″ border strips

4. Sew the long black print border strips to the side edges of the pieced quilt center. Then join the short black print border strips to the top and bottom edges of the quilt center. Press all seam allowances toward the black print border.

STICKS AND STONES

Quilt Assembly Diagram

5. Cut and piece the green print $3\frac{1}{4}\times42''$ strips to make the following:
- $2-3\frac{1}{4}\times80\frac{3}{4}''$ border strips
- $2-3\frac{1}{4}\times68\frac{1}{4}''$ border strips

6. Sew the long green print border strips to the side edges of the pieced quilt center. Then join the short green print border strips to the top and bottom edges of the quilt center. Press all seam allowances toward the green print border.

7. Sew the black floral $7\frac{1}{4}\times86\frac{1}{4}''$ strips to the side edges of the pieced quilt center. Then join the black floral $7\frac{1}{4}\times81\frac{3}{4}''$ strips to the top and bottom edges of the quilt center to complete the quilt top. Press all seam allowances toward the green print border.

Complete the Quilt

1. Layer the quilt top, batting, and backing according to the instructions in Quilting Basics, which begins *opposite*. Quilt as desired.

2. Use the black floral $2\frac{1}{2}\times42''$ strips to bind the quilt according to the instructions in Quilting Basics. ■

Quilting BASICS

GETTING STARTED

TOOLS
CUTTING
Acrylic ruler: For making perfectly straight cuts with a rotary cutter, choose a ruler of thick, clear plastic. Many sizes are available. A 6×24″ ruler marked in ¼″ increments with 30 , 45 , and 60 angles is a good first purchase.

Rotary-cutting mat: A rotary cutter should always be used with a mat designed specifically for it. In addition to protecting the table, the mat helps keep the fabric from shifting while you cut. Often these mats are described as self-healing, meaning the blade does not leave slash marks or grooves in the surface, even after repeated usage. While many shapes and styles are available, a 16×23″ mat marked with a 1″ grid, with hash marks at ⅛″ increments and 45 and 60 angles is a good choice.

Rotary cutter: The round blade of a rotary cutter will cut up to six layers of fabric at once. Because the blade is so sharp, be sure to purchase one with a safety guard and keep the guard over the blade when you're not cutting. The blade can be removed from the handle and replaced when it gets dull. Commonly available in three sizes, a good first blade is a 45mm.

Scissors: You'll need one pair for fabric and another for paper and plastic.

Pencils and other marking tools: Marks made with special quilt markers are easy to remove after sewing.

Template plastic: This slightly frosted plastic comes in sheets about ¹⁄₁₆″ thick.

PIECING
Iron and ironing board
Sewing thread: Use 100-percent-cotton thread.

Sewing machine: Any machine in good working order with well-adjusted tension will produce pucker-free patchwork seams.

APPLIQUÉ
Fusible web: Instead of the traditional method, secure cutout shapes to the background of an applique block with this iron-on adhesive.

Hand-sewing needles: For hand applique, most quilters like fine quilting needles.

HAND QUILTING
Frame or hoop: You'll get smaller, more even stitches if you stretch your quilt as you stitch. A frame supports the quilt's weight, ensures even tension, and frees both your hands for stitching. However, once set up, it cannot be disassembled until the quilting is complete. Quilting hoops are more portable and less expensive.

Quilting needles: A "between" or quilting needle is short with a small eye. Common sizes are 8, 9, and 10; size 8 is best for beginners.

Quilting thread: Quilting thread is stronger than sewing thread.

Thimble: This finger cover relieves the pressure required to push a needle through several layers of fabric and batting.

MACHINE QUILTING
Darning foot: You may find this tool, also called a hopper foot, in your sewing machine's accessory kit. If not, have the model and brand of your machine available when you go to purchase one. It is used for free-motion stitching.

Safety pins: They hold the layers together during quilting.

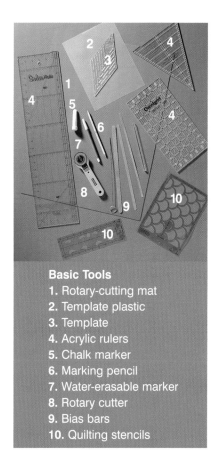

Basic Tools
1. Rotary-cutting mat
2. Template plastic
3. Template
4. Acrylic rulers
5. Chalk marker
6. Marking pencil
7. Water-erasable marker
8. Rotary cutter
9. Bias bars
10. Quilting stencils

Table: Use a large work surface that's level with your machine bed.

Thread: Use 100-percent-cotton quilting thread, cotton-wrapped polyester quilting thread, or very fine nylon monofilament thread.

Walking foot: This sewing-machine accessory helps you keep long, straight quilting lines smooth and pucker-free.

CHOOSE YOUR FABRICS
It is no surprise that most quilters prefer 100-percent-cotton fabrics for quiltmaking. Cotton fabric minimizes seam distortion, presses crisply, and is easy to quilt. Most patterns, including those in

this book, specify quantities for 44/45″-wide fabrics unless otherwise noted. Our projects call for a little extra yardage in length to allow for minor errors and slight shrinkage.

PREPARE YOUR FABRICS

There are conflicting opinions about the need to prewash fabric. The debate is a modern one because most antique quilts were made with unwashed fabric. However, the dyes and sizing used today are unlike those used a century ago.

Prewashing fabric offers quilters certainty as its main advantage. Today's fabrics resist bleeding and shrinkage, but some of both can occur in some fabrics—an unpleasant prospect once you've assembled the quilt. Some quilters find prewashed fabric easier to quilt. If you choose to prewash your fabric, press it well before cutting.

Other quilters prefer the crispness of unwashed fabric for machine piecing. And, if you use fabrics with the same fiber content throughout the quilt, then any shrinkage that occurs in its first washing should be uniform. Some quilters find this small amount of shrinkage desirable, since it gives the quilt a slightly puckered, antique look.

We recommend you prewash a scrap of each fabric to test it for shrinkage and bleeding. If you choose to prewash a fabric, unfold it to a single layer. Wash it in warm water to allow the fabric to shrink and/or bleed. If the fabric bleeds, rinse it until the water runs clear. Don't use any fabric in your quilt if it hasn't stopped bleeding. Hang fabric to dry, or tumble it in the dryer until slightly damp.

Select the Batting

For a small beginner project, a thin cotton batting is a good choice. It has a tendency to "stick" to fabric so it requires less basting. Also, it's easy to stitch. It's wise to follow the stitch density (distance between rows of stitching required to keep the batting from shifting and wadding up inside the quilt) recommendation printed on the packaging.

Polyester batting is lightweight and readily available. In general, it springs back to its original height when compressed, adding a puffiness to quilts. It tends to "beard" (work out between the weave of the fabric) more than natural fibers. Polyester fleece is denser and works well for pillow tops and place mats.

ROTARY CUTTING

Plan for Cutting

Instructions list pieces in the order in which they should be cut to make the best use of your fabrics. Always consider the fabric grain before cutting. The arrow on a pattern piece or template indicates which direction the fabric grain should run. One or more straight sides of the pattern piece or template should follow the fabric's lengthwise or crosswise grain.

The lengthwise grain, parallel to the selvage (the tightly finished edge), has the least amount of stretch. (Do not use the selvage of a woven fabric in a quilt. When washed, it may shrink more than the rest of the fabric.) Crosswise grain, perpendicular to the selvage, has a little more give. The edge of any pattern piece that will be on the outside of a block or quilt should always be cut on the lengthwise grain. Be sure to press the fabric before cutting to remove any wrinkles or folds.

Using a Rotary Cutter

When cutting, keep an even pressure on the rotary cutter and make sure the blade is touching the edge of the ruler. The less you move your fabric when cutting, the more accurate you'll be.

Squaring Up the Fabric Edge

Before rotary-cutting fabric into strips, it is imperative that one fabric edge be made straight, or squared up. Since all subsequent cuts will be measured from this straight edge, squaring up the fabric edge is an important step. There are several

Wool batting has good loft retention and absorbs moisture, making it ideal for cool, damp climates. Read the label carefully before purchasing a wool batting because it may require special handling.

different techniques for squaring up an edge, some of which involve the use of a pair of rulers. For clarity and simplicity, we have chosen to describe a single-ruler technique here. *Note:* The instructions as described are for right-handers.

1. Lay your fabric on the rotary mat with the right side down and one selvage edge away from you. Fold the fabric with the wrong side inside and the selvages together. Fold the fabric in half again, lining up the fold with the selvage edges. Lightly hand-crease all of the folds.

2. Position the folded fabric on the cutting mat with the selvage edges away from you and the bulk of the fabric length to your left. With the ruler on top of the fabric, align a horizontal grid line on the ruler with the lower folded fabric edge, leaving about 1″ of fabric exposed along the right-hand edge of the ruler (see Photo 1). Do not worry about or try to align the uneven raw edges along the right-hand side of the fabric. *Note:* If the grid lines on the cutting mat interfere with your ability to focus on the ruler grid lines, turn your cutting mat over and work on the unmarked side.

3. Hold the ruler firmly in place with your left hand, keeping your fingers away from the right-hand edge and spreading your fingers apart slightly. Apply pressure to the ruler with your fingertips to prevent it from slipping as you cut. With the ruler firmly in place, hold the rotary cutter so

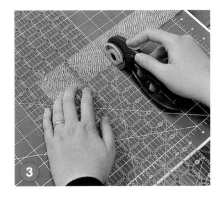

the blade is touching the right-hand edge of the ruler. Roll the blade along the ruler edge, beginning just off the folded edge and pushing the cutter away from you, toward the selvage edge.

4. The fabric strip to the right of the ruler's edge should be cut cleanly away, leaving you with a straight edge from which you can measure all subsequent cuts. Do not pick up the fabric once the edge is squared; instead, turn the cutting mat to rotate the fabric and begin cutting strips.

Cutting and Subcutting Strips
To use a rotary cutter to its greatest advantage, first cut a strip of fabric, then subcut the strip into specific sizes. For example, if your instructions say to cut forty 2″ squares, follow these steps.

1. First cut a 2″-wide strip crosswise on the fabric. Assuming you have squared up the fabric edge as described earlier, you can turn your cutting mat clockwise 180° with the newly squared-up edge on your left and the excess fabric on the right. Place the ruler on top of the fabric.

2. Align the 2″ grid mark on the ruler with the squared-up edge of the fabric (see Photo 2). Note: Align only the vertical grid mark and the fabric raw edge; ignore the selvages at the lower edge that may not line up perfectly with the horizontal ruler grid. A good rule of thumb to remember when rotary-cutting fabric is "the piece you want

to keep should be under the ruler." That way, if you accidentally swerve away from the ruler when cutting, the piece under the ruler will be "safe."

3. Placing your rotary cutter along the ruler's right-hand edge and holding the ruler firmly with your left hand, run the blade along the ruler, as in Step 3 of Squaring Up the Fabric Edge, left, to cut the strip. Remove the ruler.

4. Sliding the excess fabric out of the way, carefully turn the 2″ strip so it is horizontal on the mat. Refer to Squaring Up the Fabric Edge to trim off the selvage edges, squaring up those fabric ends.

5. Then align the 2″ grid mark on the ruler with the squared-up edge of the fabric (the 2″ square you want to keep is under the ruler). Hold the ruler with your left hand and run the rotary cutter along the right-hand ruler edge to cut a 2″ square. You can cut multiple 2″ squares from one strip by sliding the ruler over 2″ from the previous cutting line and cutting again (see Photo 3). From a 44/45″ strip, you'll likely be able to cut twenty-one 2″ squares. Since in this example you need a total of 40, cut a second 2″-wide strip and subcut it into 2″ squares.

Cutting Triangles
Right triangles also can be quickly and accurately cut with a rotary cutter. There are two common ways to cut triangles. An example of each method follows.

To cut two triangles from one square, the instructions may read:

From green print, cut:
• 20—3″ squares, cutting each in half diagonally for a total of 40 triangles

1. Referring to Cutting and Subcutting Strips, cut a 3″-wide fabric strip and subcut the strip into 3″ squares.

2. Line up the ruler's edge with opposite corners of a square to cut it in half diagonally (see Photo 4). Cut along the ruler's edge. *Note:* The triangles' resultant long edges are on the bias. Avoid stretching or overhandling these edges when piecing so that seams don't become wavy and distorted.

To cut four triangles from one square, the instructions may read:

From green print, cut:
* 20 – 6″ squares, cutting each diagonally twice in an X for a total of 80 triangles

3. Referring to Cutting and Subcutting Strips on *page 115*, cut a 6″-wide fabric strip and subcut it into 6″ squares.

4. Line up the ruler's edge with opposite corners of a square to cut it in half diagonally. Cut along the ruler's edge; do not separate the two triangles created. Line up the ruler's edge with the remaining corners and cut to make a total of four

triangles (*see page 115*). *Note:* The triangles' resultant short edges are on the bias. Avoid stretching or overhandling these edges when piecing so that seams don't become wavy and distorted.

CUTTING WITH TEMPLATES

ABOUT SCISSORS

Sharp scissor blades are vital to accurate cutting, but keeping them sharp is difficult because each use dulls the metal slightly. Cutting paper and plastic speeds the dulling process, so invest in a second pair for those materials and reserve your best scissors for fabric.

MAKE THE TEMPLATES

For some quilts, you'll need to cut out the same shape multiple times. For accurate piecing later, the individual pieces should be identical to one another.

A template is a pattern made from extra-sturdy material so you can trace around it many times without wearing away the edges. You can make your own templates by duplicating printed patterns (like those on the Pattern Sheets) on plastic.

To make permanent templates, we recommend using easy-to-cut template plastic. This material lasts indefinitely, and its transparency allows you to trace the pattern directly onto its surface.

To make a template, lay the plastic over a printed pattern. Trace the pattern onto the plastic using a ruler and a permanent marker. This will ensure straight lines, accurate corners, and permanency. Note: If the pattern you are tracing is a half-pattern to begin with, you must first make a full-size pattern. To do so, fold a piece of tracing paper in half and crease; unfold. Lay the tracing paper over the half-pattern, aligning the crease with the fold line

indicated on the pattern. Trace the half pattern. Then rotate the tracing paper, aligning the half pattern on the opposite side of the crease to trace the other half of the pattern. Use this full-size pattern to create your template.

For hand piecing and appliqué, make templates the exact size of the finished pieces, without seam allowances, by tracing the patterns' dashed lines. For machine piecing, make templates with the seam allowances included.

For easy reference, mark each template with its letter designation, grain line if noted, and block name. Verify the template's size by placing it over the printed pattern. Templates must be accurate or the error, however small, will compound many times as you assemble the quilt. To check the accuracy of your templates, make a test block before cutting the fabric pieces for an entire quilt.

Trace the Templates

To mark on fabric, use a special quilt marker that makes a thin, accurate line. Do not use a ballpoint or ink pen that may bleed if washed. Test all marking tools on a fabric scrap before using them.

To trace pieces that will be used for hand piecing or appliqué, place templates facedown on the wrong side of the fabric and trace; position the tracings at least ½″ apart (see Diagram 1, Template A). The lines drawn on the fabric are the sewing lines. Mark cutting lines, or estimate by eye a seam allowance around each piece as you

Diagram 1

cut out the pieces. For hand piecing, add a ¼″ seam allowance when cutting out the pieces; for hand appliqué, add a ³⁄₁₆″ seam allowance.

Templates used to make pieces for machine piecing have seam allowances included so you can use common lines for efficient cutting. Place templates facedown on the wrong side of the fabric and trace; position them without space in between (see Diagram 2, Template B). Using sharp scissors or a rotary cutter and ruler, cut precisely on the drawn (cutting) lines.

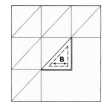

Diagram 2

Templates for Angled Pieces

When two patchwork pieces come together and form an angled opening, a third piece must be set into this angle. This happens frequently when using diamond shapes.

For a design that requires setting in, a pinhole or window template makes it easy to mark the fabric with each shape's exact sewing and cutting lines and the exact point of each corner on the sewing line. By matching the corners of adjacent pieces, you'll be able to sew them together easily and accurately.

To make a pinhole template, lay template plastic over a pattern piece. Trace both the cutting and sewing lines onto the plastic. Carefully cut out the template on the cutting line. Using a sewing-machine needle or any large needle, make a hole in the template at each corner on the sewing line (matching points). The holes must be large enough for a pencil point or other fabric marker to poke through.

Trace Angled Pieces

To mark fabric using a pinhole template, lay it facedown on the wrong side of the fabric and trace. Using a pencil, mark dots on the fabric through the holes in the template to create matching points. Cut out the fabric piece on the drawn line, making sure the matching points are marked.

To mark fabric using a window template, lay it facedown on the wrong side of the fabric (see Diagram 3). With a marking tool, mark the cutting line, sewing line, and each corner on the sewing line (matching points). Cut out the fabric piece on the cutting lines, making sure all pieces have sewing lines and matching points marked.

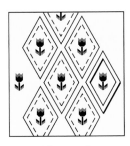

Diagram 3

HAND PIECING

In hand piecing, seams are sewn only on the marked sewing lines rather than from one raw edge to the other. Begin by matching the edges of two pieces with the right sides of the fabrics together. Sewing lines should be marked on the wrong side of both pieces. Push a pin through both fabric layers at each corner (see Diagram 1). Secure the pins perpendicular to the sewing line. Insert more pins between the corners.

Insert a needle through both fabrics at the seam-line corner. Make one or two backstitches atop the first stitch to secure the thread. Weave the needle in and out of the fabric along the seam line, taking four to six tiny stitches at a time before you pull the thread taut (see Diagram 2). Remove the pins as you sew. Turn the work over occasionally to see that the stitching follows the marked sewing line on the other side.

Sew eight to 10 stitches per inch along the seam line. At the end of the seam, remove the last pin and make the ending stitch through the hole left by the corner pin. Backstitch over the last stitch and end the seam with a loop knot (see Diagram 3).

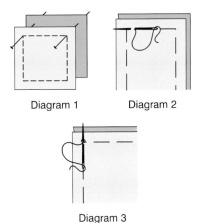

Diagram 1   Diagram 2

Diagram 3

To join rows of patchwork by hand, hold the sewn pieces with right sides together and seams matching. Insert pins at corners of the matching pieces. Add additional pins as necessary, securing each pin perpendicular to the sewing line (see Diagram 4).

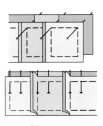

Diagram 4

Stitch the joining seam as before, but do not sew across the seam allowances that join the patches. At each seam allowance, make a backstitch or loop knot, then slide the needle through the seam allowance (see Diagram 5). Knot or backstitch again to give the intersection strength, then sew the remainder of the seam. Press each seam as it is completed.

Diagram 5

MACHINE PIECING

Machine piecing depends on sewing an exact ¼" seam allowance. Some machines have a presser foot that is the proper width, or a ¼" foot is available. To check the width of a machine's presser foot, sew a sample seam, with the raw fabric edges aligned with the right edge of the presser foot; measure the resultant seam allowance using graph paper with a ¼" grid.

Using two different thread colors one on top of the machine and one in the bobbin can help you to better match your thread color to your fabrics. If your quilt has many fabrics, use a neutral color, such as gray or beige, for both the top and bobbin threads throughout the quilt.

PRESS FOR SUCCESS

In quilting, almost every seam needs to be pressed before the piece is sewn to another, so keep your iron and ironing board near your sewing area. It's important to remember to press with an up and down motion. Moving the iron around on the fabric can distort seams, especially those sewn on the bias.

PIECING

Project instructions in this book generally tell you in what direction to press each seam. When in doubt, press both seam allowances toward the darker fabric. When joining rows of blocks, alternate the direction the seam allowances are pressed to ensure flat corners.

SETTING IN PIECES

The key to sewing angled pieces together is aligning marked matching points carefully. Whether you're stitching by machine or hand, start and stop sewing precisely at the matching points (see the dots in Diagram 6, top) and backstitch to secure the ends of the seams. This prepares the angle for the next piece to be set in.

Join two diamond pieces, sewing between matching points to make an angled unit (see Diagram 6).

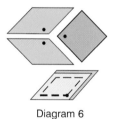

Diagram 6

Follow the specific instructions for either machine or hand piecing to complete the set-in seam.

With right sides together, pin one piece of the angled unit to one edge of the square (see Diagram 7). Match the seam's matching points by pushing a pin through both fabric layers to check the alignment. Machine-stitch the seam between the matching points. Backstitch to secure the ends of the seam; do not stitch into the ¼″ seam allowance. Remove the unit from the sewing machine.

Bring the adjacent edge of the angled unit up and align it with the next edge of the square (see Diagram 8). Insert a pin in each corner to align matching points, then pin the remainder of the seam. Machine-stitch between matching points as before. Press the seam allowances of the set-in piece away from it.

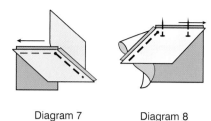

Diagram 7   Diagram 8

Pin one piece of the angled unit to one edge of the square with right sides together (see Diagram 9). Use pins to align matching points at the corners.

Hand-sew the seam from the open end of the angle into the corner. Remove pins as you sew between matching points. Backstitch at the corner to secure stitches. Do not sew into the ¼″ seam allowance and do not cut your thread.

Bring the adjacent edge of the square up and align it with the other edge of the angled unit. Insert a pin in each corner to align matching points, then pin the remainder of the seam (see Diagram 10). Hand-sew the seam from the corner to the open end of the angle, removing pins as you sew. Press the seam allowances of the set-in piece away from it.

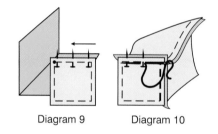

Diagram 9   Diagram 10

MITERED BORDER CORNERS

A border surrounds the piecework of many quilts. Angled, mitered corners add to a border's framed effect.

To add a border with mitered corners, first pin a border strip to a quilt top edge, matching the center of the strip and the center of the quilt top edge. Sew together, beginning and ending the seam ¼″ from the quilt top corners (see Diagram 11). Allow excess border fabric to extend beyond the edges. Repeat with remaining border strips. Press the seam allowances

toward the border strips.

Overlap the border strips at each corner (see Diagram 12). Align the edge of a 90° right triangle with the raw edge of a top border strip so the long edge of the triangle intersects the seam in the corner. With a pencil, draw along the edge of the triangle from the border seam out to the raw edge. Place the bottom border strip on top and repeat the marking process.

With the right sides of adjacent border strips together, match the marked seam lines and pin (see Diagram 13).

Beginning with a backstitch at the inside corner, stitch exactly on the marked lines to the outside edges of the border strips. Check the right side of the corner to see that it lies flat. Then trim the excess fabric, leaving a ¼″ seam allowance. Press the seam open. Mark and sew the remaining corners in this manner.

Diagram 11

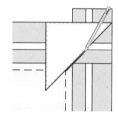

Diagram 12

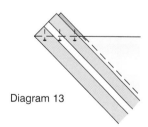

Diagram 13

APPLIQUÉ

START SIMPLE

We encourage beginners to select an appliqué design with straight lines and gentle curves. Learning to make sharp points and tiny stitches takes practice.

In the following instructions, we've used a stemmed flower motif as the appliqué example.

BASTE THE SEAM ALLOWANCES

Begin by turning under the appliqué piece 3/16" seam allowances; press. Some quilters like to thread-baste the folded edges to ensure proper placement. Edges that will be covered by other pieces don't need to be turned under.

For sharp points on tips, trim the seam allowance to within 1/8" of the stitching line (see Photo 1 opposite); taper the sides gradually to 3/16". Fold under the seam allowance remaining on the tips. Then turn the seam allowances under on both sides of the tips. The side seam allowances will overlap slightly at the tips, forming sharp points. Baste the folded edges in place (see Photo 2). The turned seam allowances may form little pleats on the back side that you also should baste in place. You'll remove the basting stitches after the shape has been appliquéd to the foundation.

MAKE BIAS STEMS

In order to curve gracefully, appliqué stems are cut on the bias. The strips for stems can be prepared in two ways. You can fold and press the strip in thirds as shown in Photo 3 opposite. Or you can fold the bias strip in half lengthwise with the wrong side inside; press. Stitch 1/4" in from the raw edges to keep them aligned. Fold the strip in half again, hiding the raw edges behind the first folded edge; press.

POSITION AND STITCH

Pin the prepared appliqué pieces in place on the foundation using the position markings or referring to the block assembly diagram (see Photo 4). If your pattern suggests it, mark the position for each piece on the foundation block before you begin. Overlap the flowers and stems as indicated.

Using thread in colors that match the fabrics, sew each stem and blossom onto the foundation with small slip stitches as shown in Photo 5. (For photographic purposes, the thread color does not match the lily.)

Catch only a few threads of the stem or flower fold with each stitch. Pull the stitches taut but not so tight that they pucker the fabric. You can use the needle's point to manipulate the appliqué edges as needed. Take an extra slip stitch at the point of a petal to secure it to the foundation.

You can use hand-quilting needles for appliqué stitching, but some quilters prefer a longer milliner's or straw needle. The extra needle length aids in tucking fabric under before taking slip stitches.

If the foundation fabric shows through the appliqué fabrics, cut away the foundation fabric. Trimming the foundation fabric also reduces the bulk of multiple layers when quilting. Carefully trim the underlying fabric to within 1/4" of the appliqué stitches (see Photo 6). Do not cut the appliqué fabric.

FUSIBLE APPLIQUÉ

For quick-finish appliqué, use paper-backed fusible web. Then you can iron the shapes onto the foundation and add decorative stitching to the edges. This product consists of two layers, a fusible webbing lightly bonded to paper that peels off. The webbing adds a slight stiffness to the back of the appliqué pieces.

When you purchase this product, read the directions on the bolt end or packaging to make sure you're buying the right kind for your project. Some brands are specifically engineered to bond fabrics with no sewing at all. If you try to stitch fabric after it has bonded with one of these products, you may encounter difficulty. Some paper-backed fusible products are made exclusively for sewn edges; others work with or without stitching.

If you buy paper-backed fusible web from a bolt, be sure fusing instructions are included because the iron temperature and timing varies by brand. This information is usually on the paper backing.

APPLIQUE

With any of these products, the general procedure is to trace the pattern wrong side up onto the paper side of the fusible web. Then place the fusible web on the wrong side of the appliqué fabrics, paper side up, and use an iron to fuse the layers together. Then cut out the shapes, peel off the paper, turn the fabrics right side up, and fuse the shapes to the foundation fabric.

You also can fuse the fusible web and fabric together before tracing. You'll still need to trace templates wrong side up on the paper backing.

If you've used a no-sew fusible web, your appliqué is done. If not, finish the edges with hand or machine stitching.

CUTTING BIAS STRIPS

Strips for curved appliqué pattern pieces, such as meandering vines, and for binding curved edges should be cut on the bias (diagonally across the grain of a woven fabric), which runs at a 45° angle to the selvage and has the most give or stretch.

To cut bias strips, begin with a fabric square or rectangle. Use a large acrylic ruler to square up the left edge of the fabric. Make the first cut at a 45° angle to the left edge (see Bias Strip Diagram). Handle the diagonal edges carefully to avoid distorting the bias. To cut a strip, measure the desired width parallel to the 45° cut edge; cut. Continue cutting enough strips to total the length needed.

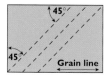

Bias Strip Diagram

COVERED CORDING

Covered cording is made by sewing a bias-cut fabric strip around a length of cording. The width of the bias strip will vary depending on the diameter of your cording. Refer to the specific project instructions for those measurements. Regardless, the method used to cover the cording is the same.

With the wrong side inside, fold under 1½" at one end of the bias strip. With the wrong side inside, fold the strip in half lengthwise to make the cording cover. Insert the cording next to the folded edge, placing a cording end 1" from the cording cover folded end. Using a machine cording foot, sew through both fabric layers right next to the cording (see Diagram 1).

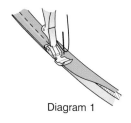

Diagram 1

When attaching the cording to your project, begin stitching 1½" from the covered cording's folded end. Round the corners slightly, making sure the corner curves match. As you stitch each corner, gently ease the covered cording into place (see Diagram 2).

HANGING SLEEVES

Quilts make wonderful pieces of wall art. When treated as museum pieces and hung properly, they won't deteriorate. Let size be your guide when determining how to hang your quilt.

Hang smaller quilts, a 25" square or less, with purchased clips, sewn-on tabs, or pins applied to the corners. Larger quilts require a hanging sleeve attached to the back. It may take a few minutes more to sew on a sleeve, but the effort preserves your hours of work with less distortion and damage.

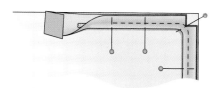

Diagram 2

After going around the entire edge of the project, cut the end of the cording so that it will fit snugly into the folded opening at the beginning (see Diagram 3). The ends of the cording should abut inside the covering. Stitch the ends in place to secure (see Diagram 4).

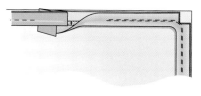

Diagram 3

Diagram 4

MAKE A HANGING SLEEVE

1. Measure the quilt's top edge.

2. Cut a 6"- to 10"-wide strip of prewashed fabric 2" longer than the quilt's top edge. For example, if the top edge is 40", cut a 6×42" strip. A 6"-wide strip is sufficient for a dowel or drapery rod. If you're using something bigger in diameter, cut a wider fabric strip. If you're sending your quilt to be displayed at a quilt show, adjust your measurements to accommodate the show's requirements.

3. Fold under 1½" on both short ends of the fabric strip. Sew ¼" from raw edges (see Diagram 1).

Diagram 1

4. Fold the fabric strip in half lengthwise with the wrong side inside; pin. Stitch together the long edges with a ¼" seam allowance (see Diagram 2) to make the sleeve. Press the seam allowance open and center the seam in the middle of the sleeve (see Diagram 3).

Diagram 2

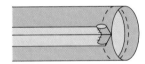

Diagram 3

5. Center the sleeve on the quilt backing about 1" below the binding with the seam facing the backing (see Diagram 4). Stitching through the backing and batting, slip-stitch the sleeve to the quilt along both long edges and the portions of the short edges that touch the backing.

Diagram 4

6. Slide a wooden dowel or slender piece of wood that is 1" longer than the finished sleeve into the sleeve and hang as desired.

LAYERING

Cut and piece the backing fabric to measure at least 3" bigger on all sides than the quilt top. Press all seam allowances open. with wrong sides together, layer the quilt top and backing fabric with the batting in between; baste. Quilt as desired.

BINDING

The binding for most quilts is cut on the straight grain of the fabric. If your quilt has curved edges, cut the strips on the bias (*opposite*). The cutting instructions for projects in this book specify the number of binding strips or a total length needed to finish the quilt. The instructions also specify enough width for a French-fold or double-layer binding because it's easier to apply and adds durability.

Join the strips with diagonal seams to make one continuous binding strip (see Diagram 1). Trim the excess fabric, leaving ¼" seam allowances. Press the seam allowances open. Then, with the wrong sides together, fold under 1" at one end of the binding strip (see Diagram 2); press. Fold the strip in half lengthwise (see Diagram 3); press.

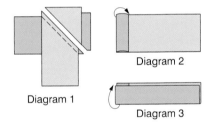

Diagram 1

Diagram 2

Diagram 3

Beginning in the center of one side, place the binding strip against the right side of the quilt top, aligning the binding strip's raw edges with the quilt top's raw edge (see Diagram 4). Beginning 1½" from the folded edge, sew through all layers, stopping ¼" from the corner. Backstitch, then clip the threads. Remove the quilt from under the sewing-machine presser foot.

Fold the binding strip upward (see Diagram 5), creating a diagonal fold, and finger-press.

Holding the diagonal fold in place with your finger, bring the binding strip down

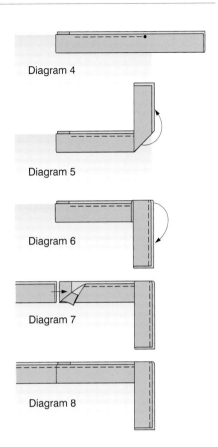

Diagram 4

Diagram 5

Diagram 6

Diagram 7

Diagram 8

in line with the next edge, making a horizontal fold that aligns with the top edge of the quilt (see Diagram 6).

Start sewing again at the top of the horizontal fold, stitching through all layers. Sew around the quilt, turning each corner in the same manner.

When you return to the starting point, lap the binding strip inside the beginning fold (see Diagram 7). Finish sewing to the starting point (see Diagram 8). Trim the batting and backing fabric even with the quilt top edges.

Turn the binding over the edge of the quilt to the back. Hand-stitch the binding to the backing fabric, making sure to cover any machine stitching.

To make mitered corners on the back, hand-stitch the binding up to a corner; fold a miter in the binding. Take a stitch or two in the fold to secure it. Then stitch the binding in place up to the next corner. Finish each corner in the same manner. ■

PATTERNS

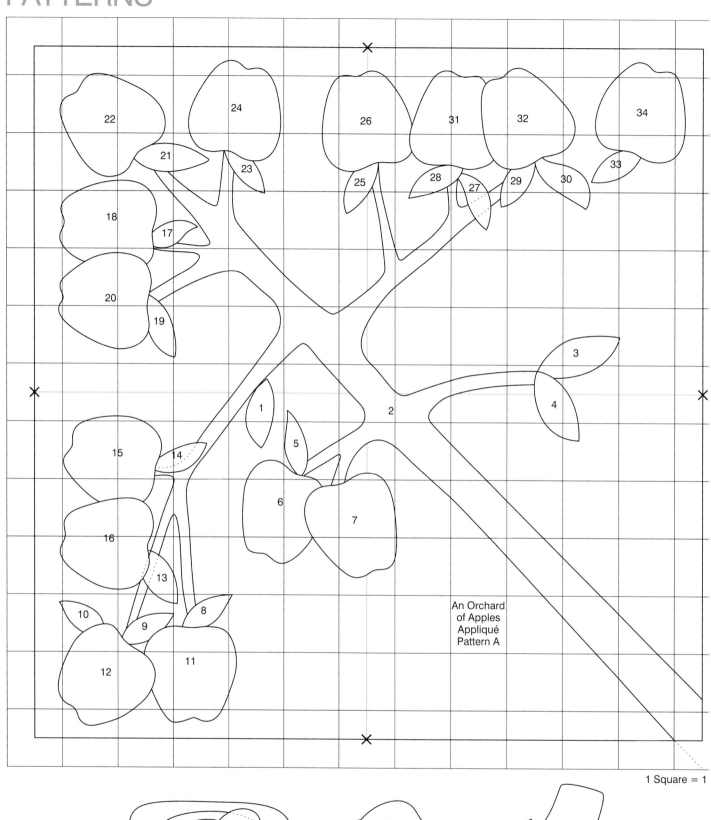

22 21 24 23 26 31 32 34 25 28 27 29 30 33 18 17 20 19 3 4 1 5 2 15 14 6 7 16 13 10 8 9 12 11

An Orchard
of Apples
Appliqué
Pattern A

1 Square = 1

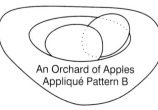

An Orchard of Apples
Appliqué Pattern B

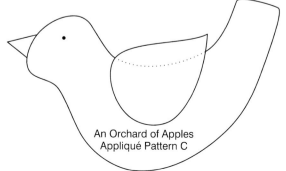

An Orchard of Apples
Appliqué Pattern C

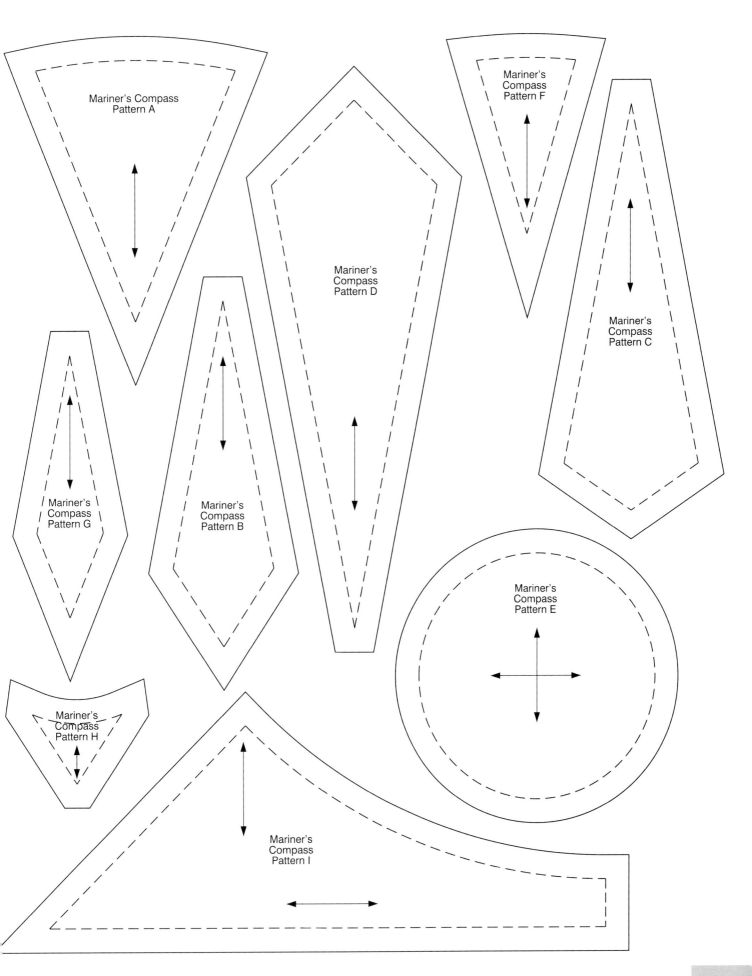

Mariner's Compass Pattern A

Mariner's Compass Pattern F

Mariner's Compass Pattern C

Mariner's Compass Pattern D

Mariner's Compass Pattern G

Mariner's Compass Pattern B

Mariner's Compass Pattern E

Mariner's Compass Pattern H

Mariner's Compass Pattern I

PATTERNS

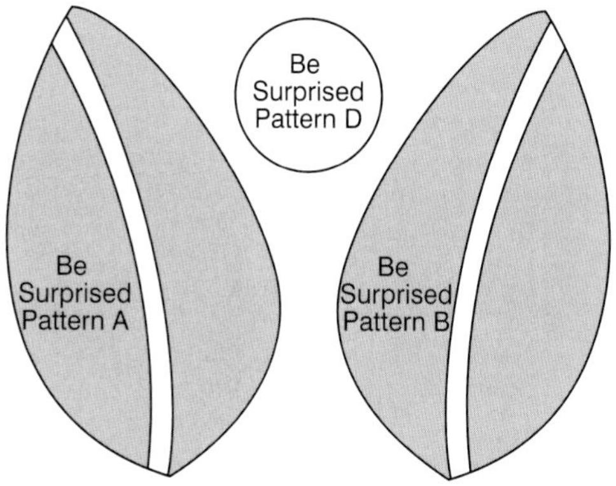

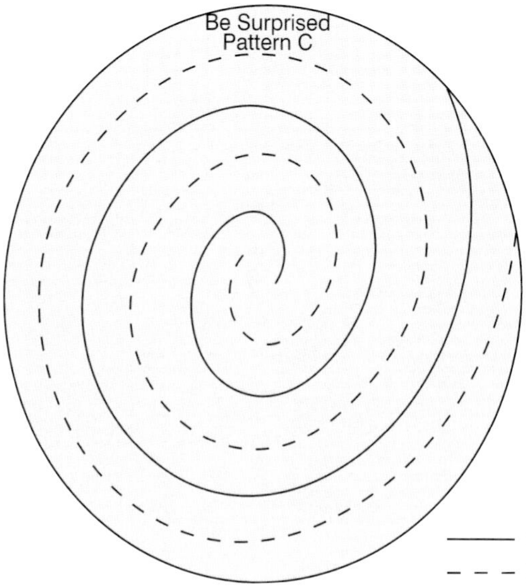

Be Surprised
Pattern D

Be
Surprised
Pattern A

Be
Surprised
Pattern B

Be Surprised
Pattern C

——— Cutting line
– – – Basting line

| Purple Backstitch – lettering
• Purple French Knot – lettering
| Green Backstitch – vines, flower center circles
⬭ Green Lazy Daisy Stitch – leaves

▥ Purple Satin Stitch – flower petals
⌒ Purple Fly Stitch – flower petals
◉ Yellow (1X) and Green (1X) French Knot – flower centers
○ Yellow French Knot – tip of flower petals

Love wholeheartedly, be surprised, and give thanks.

Be Surprised
Center Embroidery Pattern

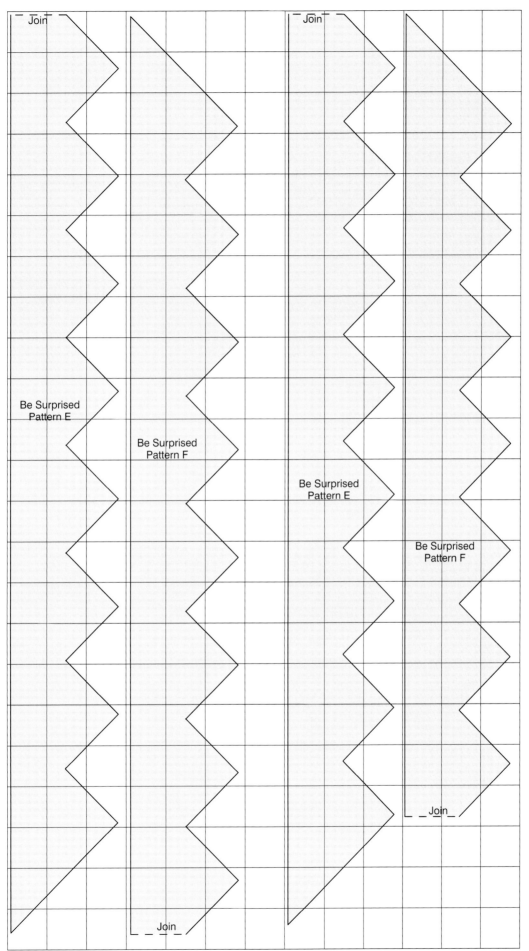

Join

Be Surprised
Pattern E

Be Surprised
Pattern F

Join

Be Surprised
Pattern E

Be Surprised
Pattern F

Join

Join

1 Square = 1/2-inch

PATTERNS

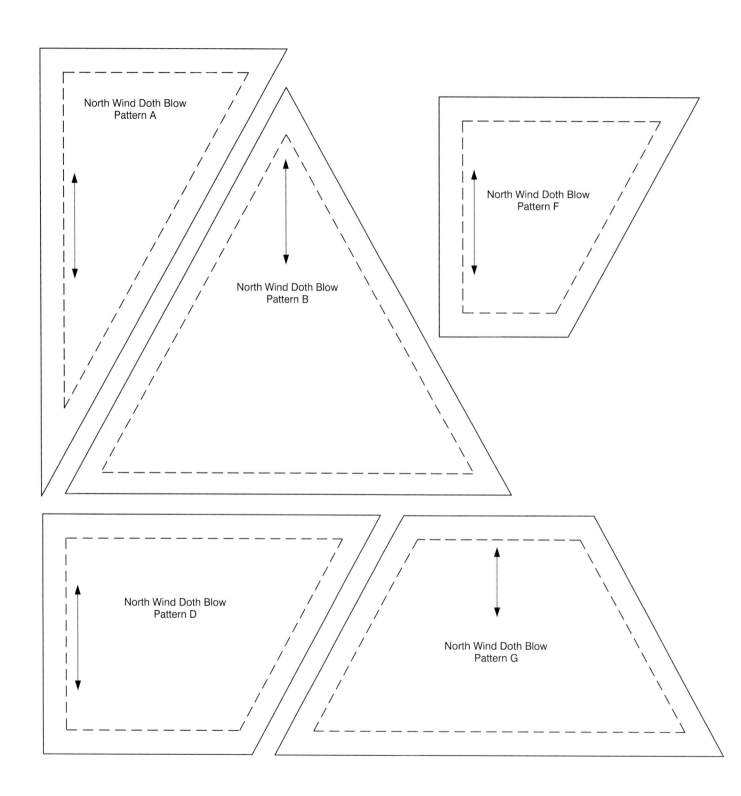

North Wind Doth Blow
Pattern A

North Wind Doth Blow
Pattern B

North Wind Doth Blow
Pattern F

North Wind Doth Blow
Pattern D

North Wind Doth Blow
Pattern G

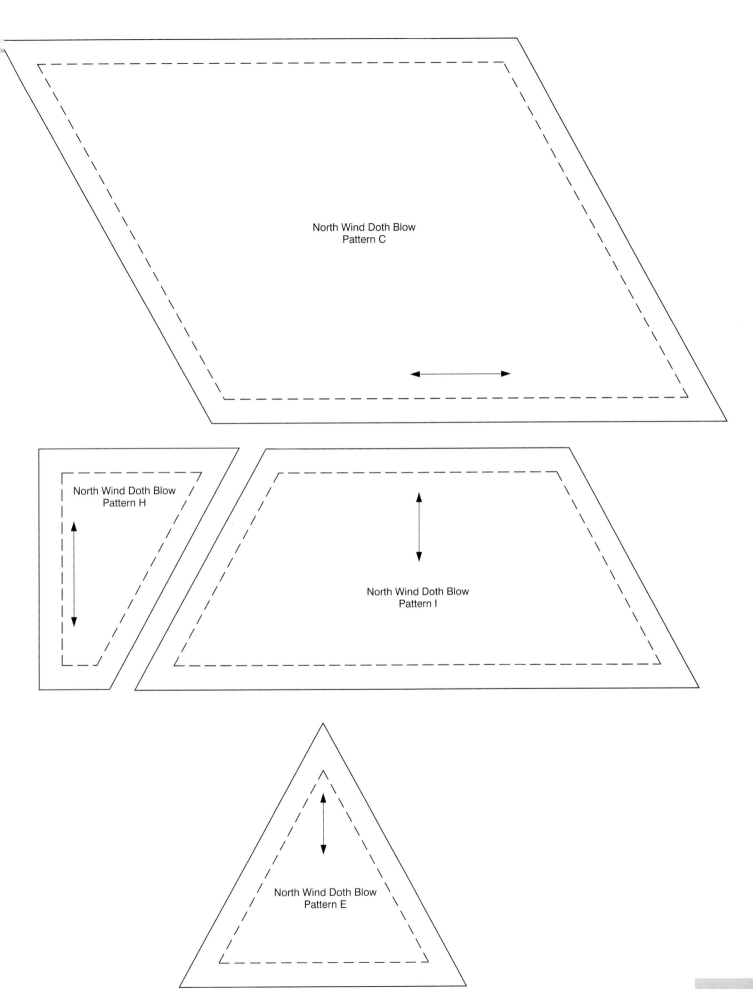

North Wind Doth Blow
Pattern C

North Wind Doth Blow
Pattern H

North Wind Doth Blow
Pattern I

North Wind Doth Blow
Pattern E

PATTERNS

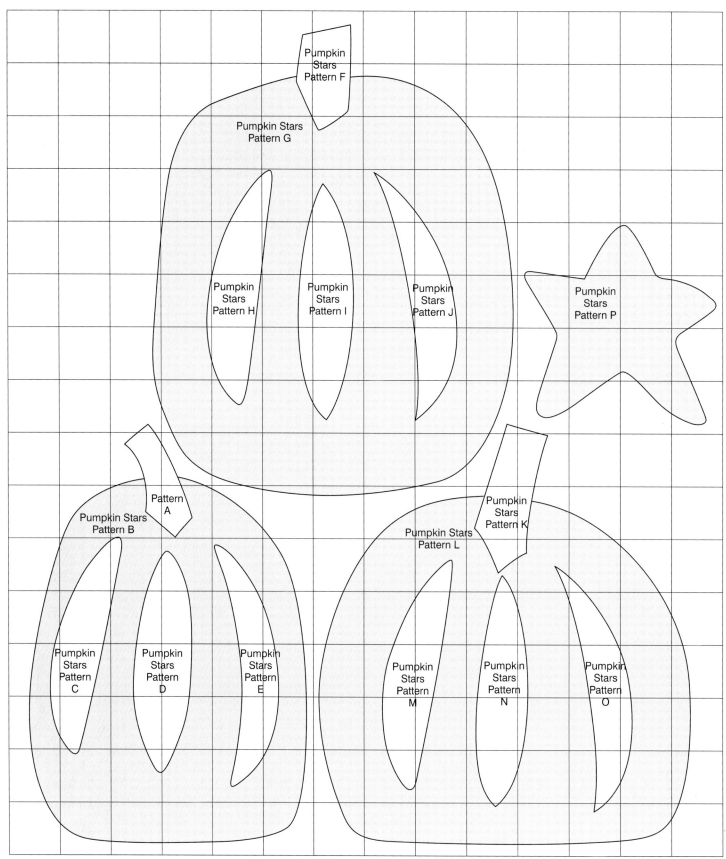

Pumpkin Stars Pattern F

Pumpkin Stars Pattern G

Pumpkin Stars Pattern H

Pumpkin Stars Pattern I

Pumpkin Stars Pattern J

Pumpkin Stars Pattern P

Pattern A

Pumpkin Stars Pattern B

Pumpkin Stars Pattern C

Pumpkin Stars Pattern D

Pumpkin Stars Pattern E

Pumpkin Stars Pattern K

Pumpkin Stars Pattern L

Pumpkin Stars Pattern M

Pumpkin Stars Pattern N

Pumpkin Stars Pattern O

1 Square = 1 Inch